CONTENTS

 @lfc   @liverpoolfc  liverpoolfc  @liverpoolfc

Editor William Hughes **Writer** Chris McLoughlin **Production** Michael McGuinness, Roy Gilfoyle, Adam Oldfield **Design** Colin Sumpter, Chris Collins, Adam Ward **Photography** Alamy, Mirrorpix, Liverpool Echo, John Powell, Andrew Powell, Nicholas Taylor, Nikki Dyer © Liverpool Football Club & Athletic Grounds Ltd **Published by** Reach Sport
Art Editor Colin Sumpter **Marketing & Communications Manager** Claire Brown
Website www.reachsportshop.com **Printed by** Buxton Press

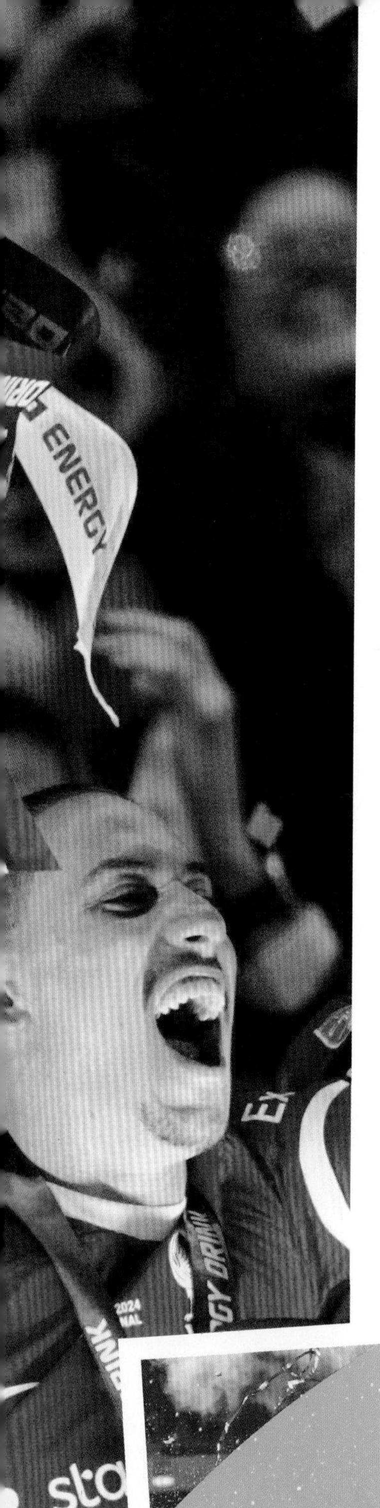

PERFECT TEN

A record-extending Carabao Cup triumph is marked with scenes of ecstasy and euphoria at Wembley as Klopp's rousing Reds secure their first piece of silverware of the 2023/24 season

standard chartered
Expedia
Carabao ENERGY DRINK

Expedia
standard chartered
Carabao ENERGY DRINK

ENERGY DRINK

Carabao
ENERGY DRINK

LIVERPOOL FC
YOU'LL NEVER WALK ALONE

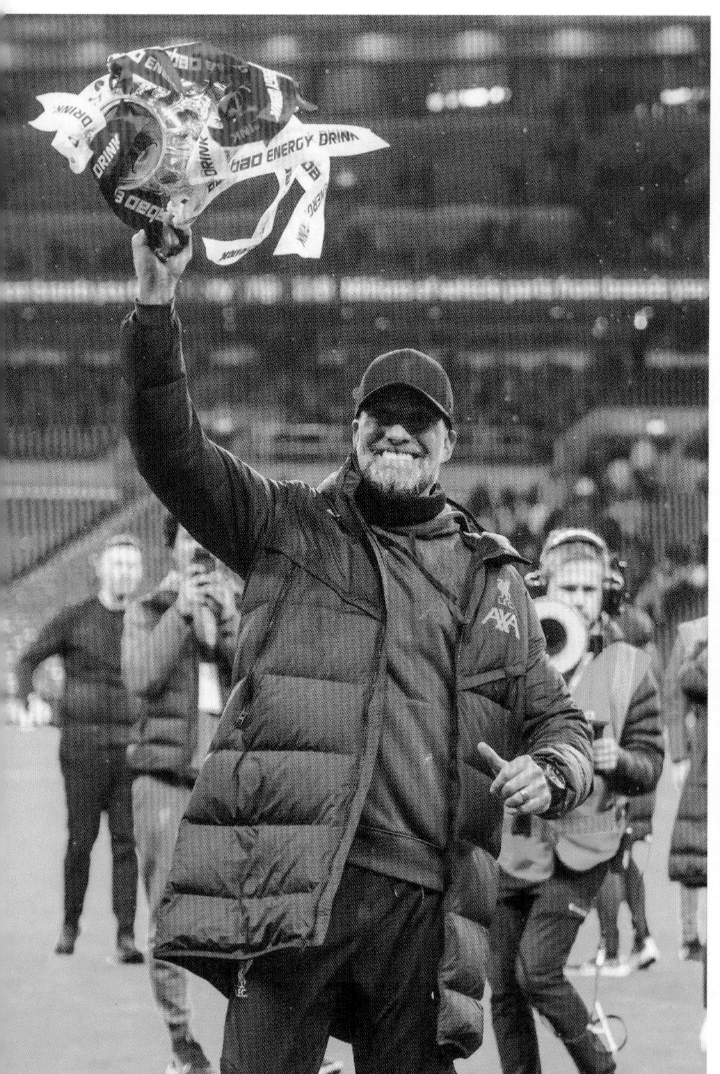

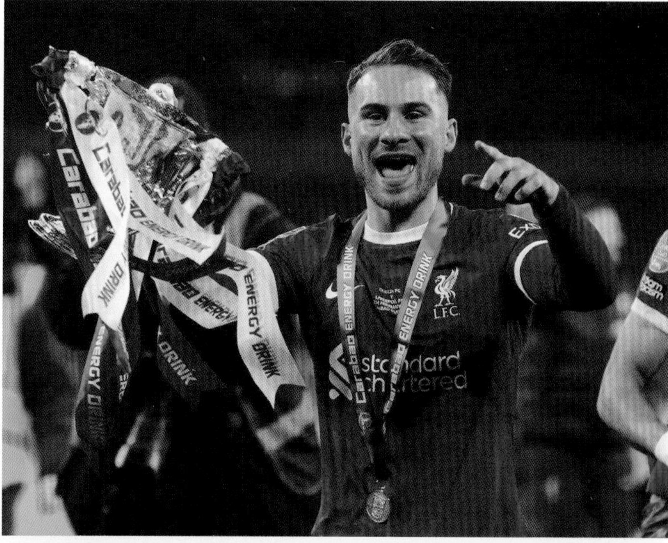

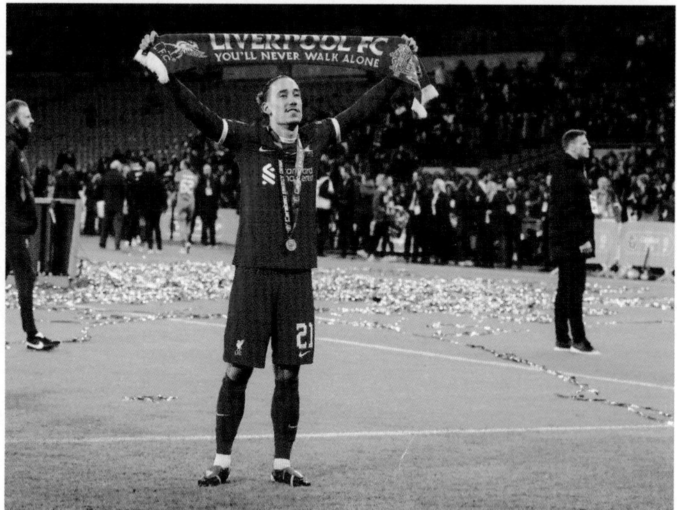

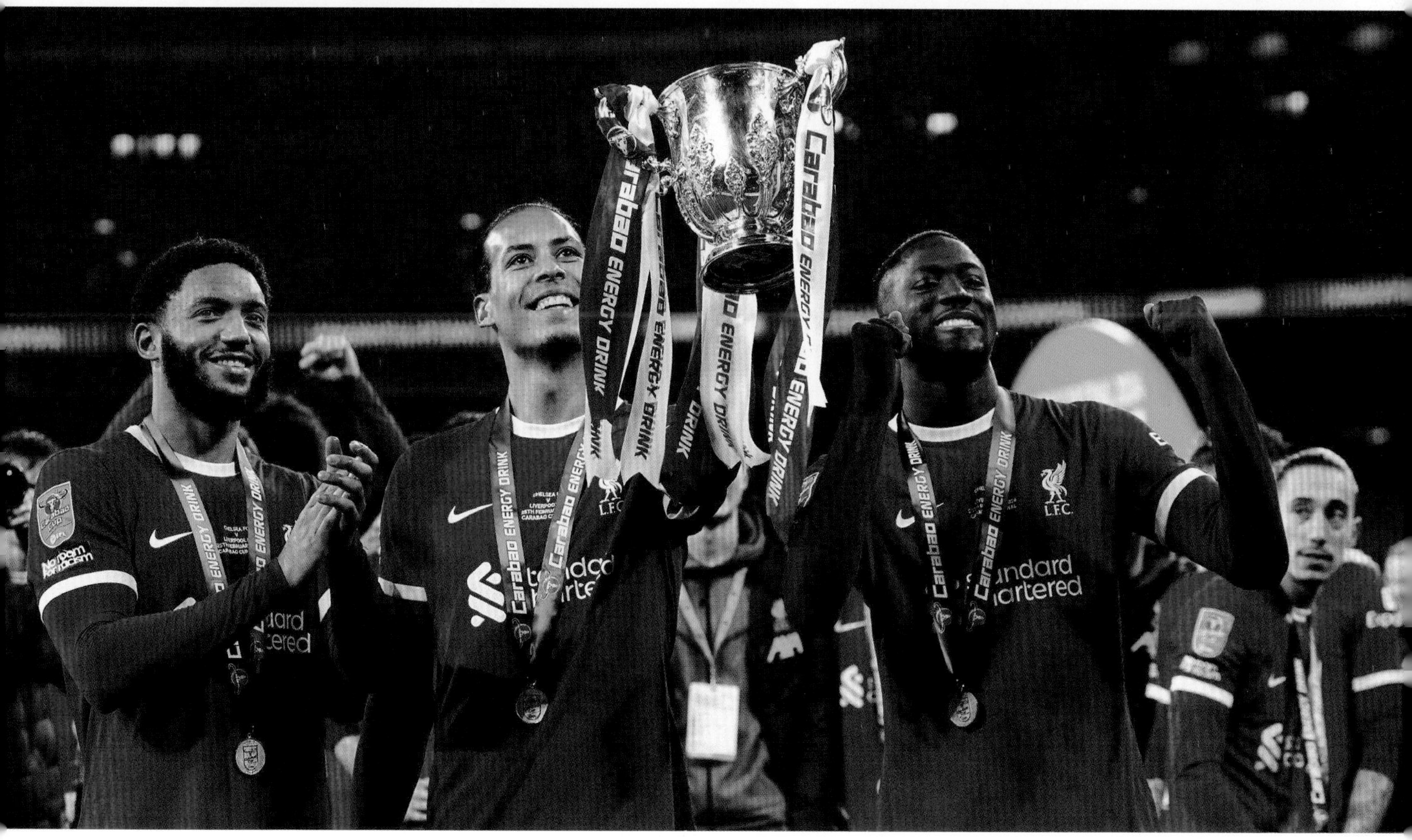
Carabao ENERGY DRINK
L.F.C.
Standard Chartered

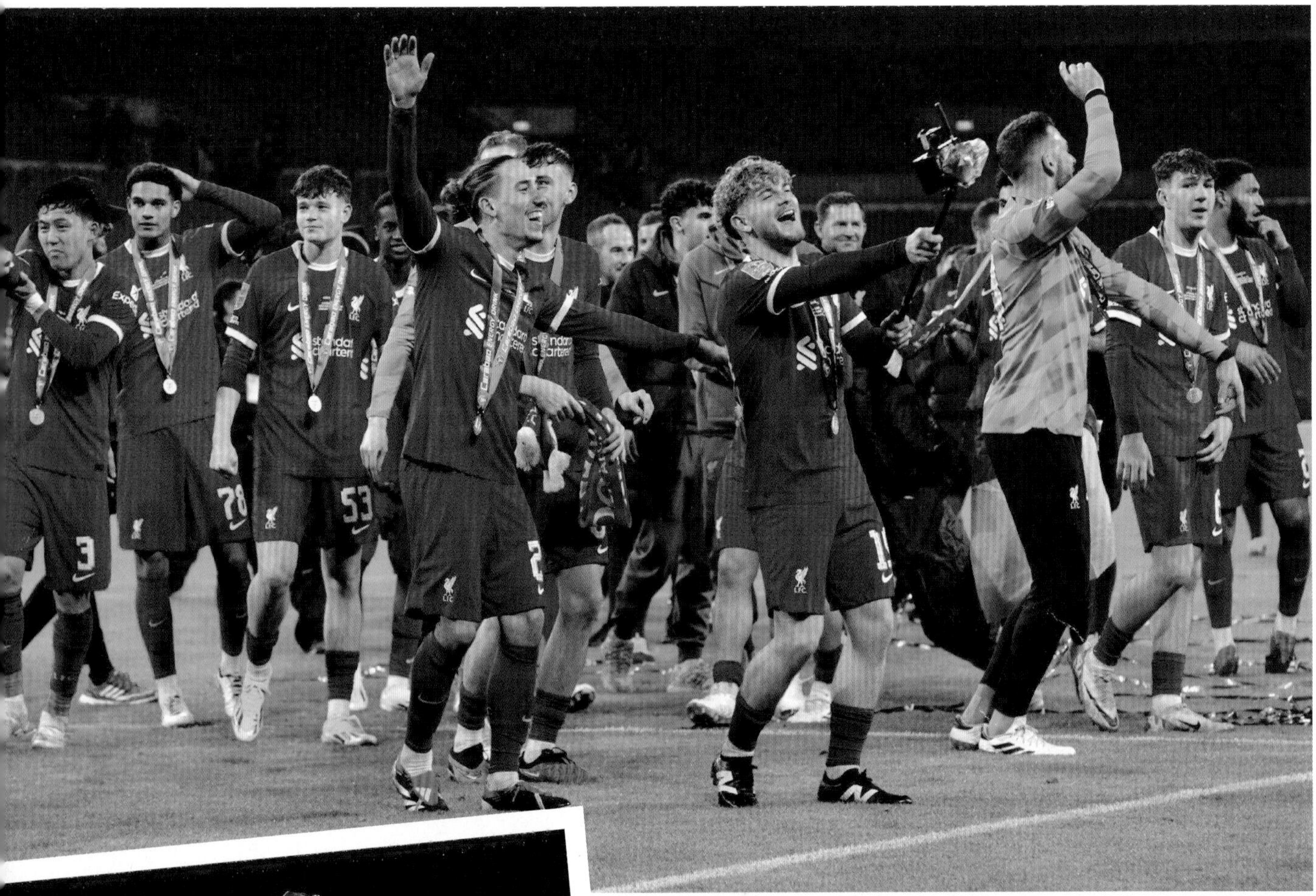

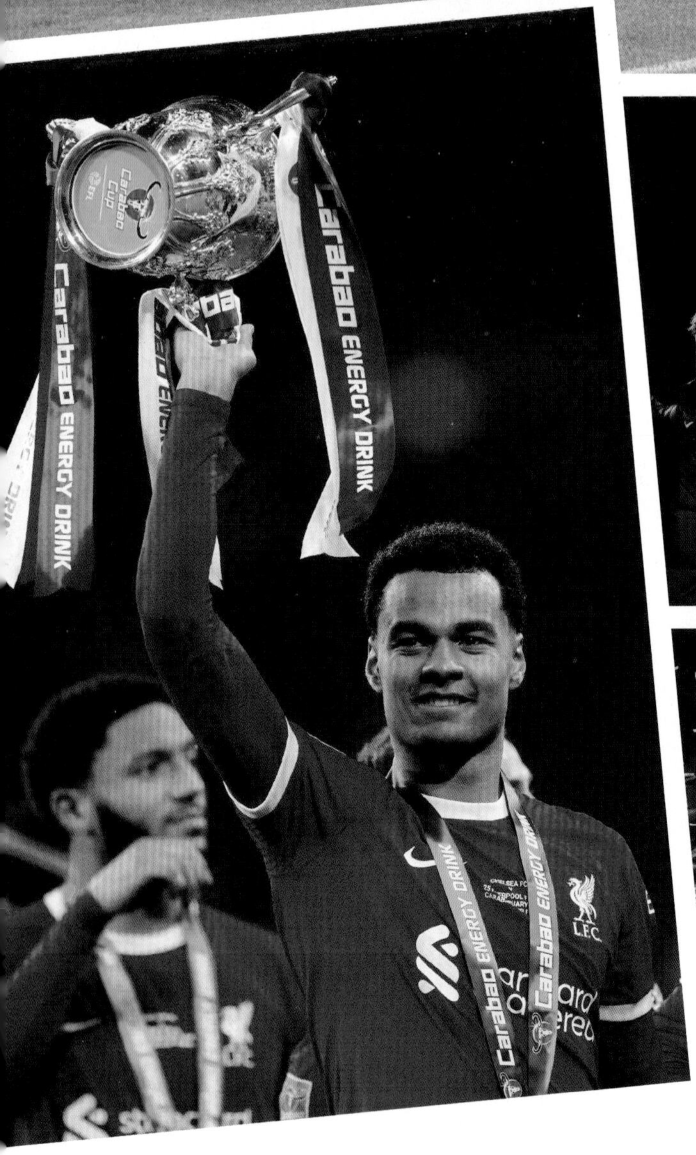
Carabao ENERGY DRINK
Carabao ENERGY DRINK

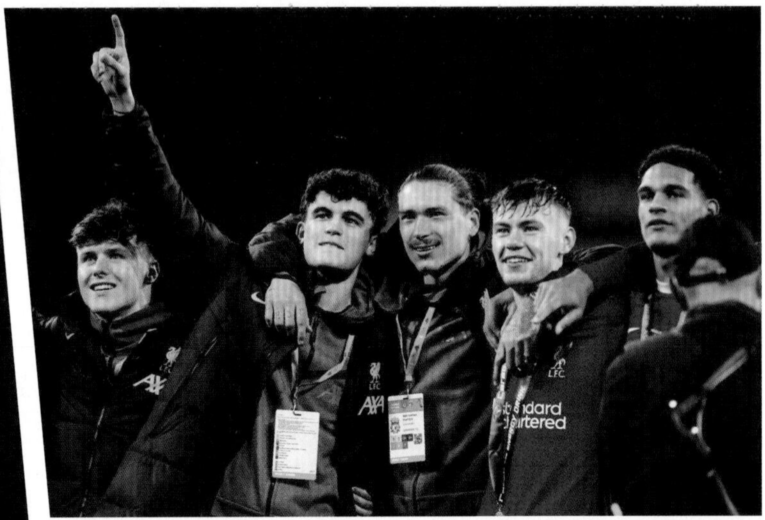

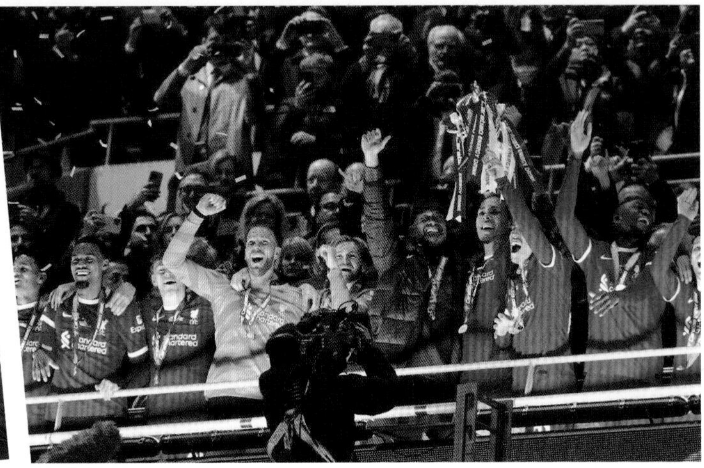

AXA

Carabao Cup
EFL
standard chartered
Carabao ENERGY DRINK

standard chartered

Carabao ENERGY DRINK
AXA

standard chartered
Carabao ENERGY DRINK

'There are longer careers than mine but in more than 20 years, [it's easily] the most special trophy I ever won'

THE MANAGER SPEAKS...

JÜRGEN KLOPP

"What we saw here today is so exceptional. We might never see it again and not because I am on the sideline, but because these things don't happen in football. I got told outside that there's an English phrase, 'You don't win trophies with kids' – I didn't know that. Yeah?! There are longer careers than mine but in more than 20 years, [it's] easily the most special trophy I ever won. It's absolutely exceptional. Sometimes I get asked if I'm proud of this, proud of that, proud of that, and it's really tricky. I wish I could feel pride more often, I just don't. Tonight though, there's an overwhelming feeling, 'Oh my God, what's going on here?' I was proud of everybody involved in everything here.

I was proud of our people for the way they pushed us. I was proud of the staff for creating this kind of atmosphere surrounding where these boys can just do what they are best at. I was proud of our Academy. I was proud of my coaches. I was proud of so many things. It was really overwhelming. It had nothing to do with maybe my last game at Wembley – I checked that, nothing to do with that. It was really because of how everybody contributed, seeing the faces after the game of the kids – Jayden Danns. Can you create in football stories which definitely nobody will ever forget? It's so difficult because this happened before, this happened before, they won it then, there. If you find the same story with academy players coming on against a top, top, top side and still winning it, I never heard it.

"This was so special. You saw the game, you saw the circumstances. We had problems before the game, they became bigger during the game... And then getting through all of this, you see tired players. For tonight it is a night I will never forget. If nobody else sees it like that, no problem. For me, it's a really nice memory, forever."

WORDS FROM OUR WEMBLEY WINNERS

A host of the Reds' triumphant squad spoke to Sky Sports following the win over Chelsea. Here's what they had to say:

VIRGIL VAN DIJK

Matchwinner Virgil van Dijk spoke of his immense pride in his team after his first trophy lift as Liverpool captain.

The Dutchman headed in the 118th minute winner having earlier thought he had broken the deadlock only to be denied by a VAR review.

The no4 was also named player of the match, becoming the fourth man to win the Alan Hardaker Trophy on two occasions following in the footsteps of Ben Foster, John Terry and Vincent Kompany.

"All the young boys on the pitch, if you see the extra-time, it's incredible. I'm so proud of the team," he told Sky Sports.

"An intense game for both sides, they had chances, we had chances and [it's] amazing. First trophy as the Liverpool captain – it's all for the fans so let's enjoy it.

"You should always savour the good moments and this is definitely one of them. We will never take these things for granted, we are very, very blessed and you see today as well that it could have been the other way, we could have lost. But we didn't, we did the job, even with all the problems that we had before the game and during the game – and yeah, I am so proud. I'm always proud to be part of this club but especially proud of the boys. They all played their part so it's all credit to the team."

Van Dijk also revealed that he requested that manager Jürgen Klopp join him for the trophy presentation.

"I wanted him to be next to me and I'm happy that he agreed. It's a proud moment, a special moment and something I will cherish forever.

"Let's hope [this is] a big platform. We need everyone until the end of the season. But we are in everything so why not just go out and enjoy it? All of us, not only the players – staff, but especially the fans.

"It's a beautiful time – and we have to not take these times for granted. We have to go for it and do it all together. That's what I'm looking forward to."

ANDY ROBERTSON

"When you get to these finals you want to be on the winning side because you've worked all year to get here and you want to send your fans back home happy. I think we've done that today.

"It's always nice to get a trophy. Everyone knows the manager is leaving and I think this one meant a lot to him, especially with so many players out and him putting trust in the young players. We're just happy to produce a trophy for him and all the staff who are leaving at the end of the season.

"When the squads were announced some outsiders probably wrote us off because we've got too many players missing, but we knew the quality we had in that changing room.

"We went with everything we had and the young lads came on and made such a difference. They enjoyed every moment of it and that's what we told them to do - don't be scared of it, go and relish it. They all did that, it was a real collective performance.

"It's not ideal the amount of players we've got injured and I think the rest of us need to get wrapped in cotton wool! But we ended up with a pretty young team out there and the big man popped up with the winner.

"I'm not sure his first goal should have been chalked off. It was frustrating, but it is what it is and Virg had his shooting boots on - well his heading boots, even - and thought 'I've done it once, why not do it again?' It was a great header from him so late on in his game.

"Caoimh was different class and I think if Virg doesn't score the winner he gets man-of-the-match. His distribution was excellent, his saving was excellent and to keep a clean sheet in a final - you can't ask much more than that. He's an unbelievable character around the squad and so important to what we do."

CAOIMHIN KELLEHER

"These are the moments you dream about. It's better for the heart than penalties! Another amazing moment for me, I'm delighted.

"Virgil is unbelievable, he is always fit, always showing up for us. He is pushing us on to win more trophies."

"We won't get ahead of ourselves, but this is great for momentum. We are in a good place right now."

CONOR BRADLEY

"I don't think I can actually put it into words. It's an incredible feeling and obviously I've supported this club since I was about five-years-old so to now win a trophy with them at Wembley, it's special and I'm just buzzing.

"Thankfully I wasn't on at the end because I don't know if I could have kept my composure! The boys did brilliant and especially the young ones that came on, they showed real heart and they always wanted the ball and they always wanted to make something happen. So, full credit to the boys.

"Obviously we were all looking forward to it. It's a massive game for us, especially the young ones. But obviously it wasn't easy with the amount of injuries we did have but we're just so thankful to get over the line and get the win, and get the win for the manager.

"I think it all comes from the gaffer, to be honest, the confidence that he puts in us youngsters. He just tells us to go out there and enjoy it and that's what we try to do and we're so happy to get the win today.

"It makes it much easier coming into the first team whenever the Under-21s and the Under-18s all play the same way, so you know what you are doing whenever you do get thrown in and it obviously makes it a lot easier. The work that goes in at the Academy is brilliant."

LUIS DIAZ

"It was a very tough match and big matches are played this way. We have a year with lots of matches, prepare like that for every game. We knew it would be a challenge but we prepared really well.

"I dedicate this title to my mum and dad for everything they have been through. It means a lot to be able to celebrate with them."

BOBBY CLARK

"When he [Jürgen Klopp] called my name and said I was going on it was an unbelievable feeling. He fills you with confidence, gives you freedom, really lets you do your thing."

TEN TIMES TABLED

CHELSEA 0
LIVERPOOL 1 (after extra-time)

25.02.24 • Wembley • Attendance: 88,868

Referee: Chris Kavanagh

REPORT BY WILLIAM HUGHES

CHELSEA (4-2-3-1): Petrovic; Gusto, Disasi, Colwill, Chilwell (C) (Chalobah 113); Caicedo, Fernandez; Palmer, Gallagher (Madueke 97), Sterling (Nkunku 66); Jackson (Mudryk 90).
Subs not used: Sanchez, Bettinelli, Chalobah, Gilchrist, Gee, Tuariainen.
Booked: Chilwell, Palmer.

LIVERPOOL (4-3-3): Kelleher; Bradley (Clark 72), Konate (Quansah 106), van Dijk (C), Robertson (Tsimikas 86); Endo, Mac Allister (McConnell 86), Gravenberch (Gomez 28); Elliott, Gakpo (Danns 86), Diaz.
Subs not used: Adrian, Nyoni, Koumas.
Booked: Bradley, Mac Allister, Konate, McConnell, Gomez.

PRESS BOX: DAVID HYTNER, THE GUARDIAN
"Here Klopp's team were fighting until the last breath. It was Liverpool who found the purpose and clarity in the extra period. Klopp's scriptwriter had something left, the detail to ignite his quest to collect four more trophies before he rides off into the sunset at the end of the season. The celebrations would be suitably wild upon the full-time whistle, Klopp's punches to the Liverpool supporters heavy on emotion. The photographers got the picture they wanted when Klopp and Van Dijk lifted the trophy together and there was a

scene that quickly went viral when Klopp, every Liverpool player and every member of staff draped arms around each other and swayed in one line to the strains of You'll Never Walk Alone."

PUNDIT: JAMIE REDKNAPP, SKY SPORTS
"When you work with elite players, like Alisson, it rubs off on you. You can think what's the point in training all the time when you know you have a world class player in front of you. Caoimhin Kelleher deserves so much credit, he is so resilient and you have to have such a great attitude for every occasion and he deserves it."

FOR THE RECORD:
Virgil van Dijk has scored in 21 games for Liverpool and won every single time - the most games a player has ever scored in for the Reds while winning 100% of them.

REPORT:
As Jürgen Klopp has said many times: 'Wow!' Liverpool's victory in the Carabao Cup final saw them become the first club to take their trophy count in the tournament into double figures - but few of their previous successes will have tasted as sweet as this.

There were a host of sub-plots in an enthralling final but the main storyline was that of how a Liverpool team that played extra-time with three teenage rookies on the field - and another player aged under 21 - managed to hold their nerve to overcome Chelsea at Wembley for the third time in three seasons.

In recent weeks, Klopp has paid tribute to the cluster of youngsters helping the Reds through a turbulent time during which he has been without a whole starting eleven sidelined through injuries.

"We wouldn't be where we are without them," he acknowledged. The manager's faith has been telling but, as they have shown time and again already, the kids are alright.

It needed extra-time. Of course it did. But there was a sense of poetic justice that it was Virgil van Dijk, Liverpool's leader, who was the Reds' match-winner.

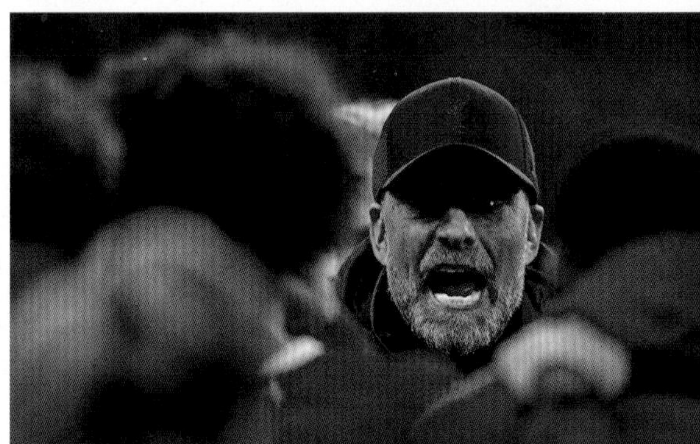

The captain had been denied what he thought was a perfectly good goal to break the deadlock on the hour mark when referee Chris Kavanagh was sent to the VAR screen. After numerous replays of near-forensic study of slow motion replays, the official decided that Wataru Endo was offside when he blocked Blues defender Levi Colwill from making a challenge after Andy Robertson's free-kick was headed home by the Dutchman.

In fairness, Liverpool had enjoyed a let-off of their own after 32 minutes when Chelsea striker Nicolas Jackson broke down the right and squared for ex-Reds winger Raheem Sterling to tap home at the far post. When the VAR lines were drawn, Jackson's knee was adjudged to have been fractionally in advance of Ibrahima Konate's.

The stalemate was also preserved until deep into extra-time by three efforts which struck the base of the post.

Five minutes before half-time, Chelsea centre-back Axel Disasi lost control down the right and the ball was worked to Andy Robertson. His cross was slightly behind Cody Gakpo but the Dutchman flexed his neck muscles to direct the ball out of the reach of goalkeeper Djordje Petrovic but against the woodwork.

Fifteen minutes before the end of the regulation 90, it was Chelsea's turn to be denied. The impressive Cole Palmer picked out fellow midfielder Conor Gallagher and his shot found the frame of the goal.

Liverpool fans behind the goal at the at the East end of the stadium were off their feet five minutes before the end of extra-time when substitute Kostas Tsimikas produced a fine cross to pick out Harvey Elliott's run to the far post but the 20-year old's header also rebounded off the post before being scrambled clear by the Chelsea defence.

Tsimikas was not to be denied his assist, however. Three minutes later and with the spectre of a third successive Wembley penalty contest looming large, one of the Reds' three teenage substitutes, Bobby Clark, worked space for a shot which was deflected over the bar.

Tsimikas, Liverpool's shoot-out matchwinner in the FA Cup final in 2022, delivered a fine corner and there was Van Dijk to get in front of his marker and provide the game's decisive touch, finding the corner of Petrovic's goal.

Clark had been joined on the pitch by fellow teenagers James McConnell and Jayden Danns towards the end of normal time. The latter had only made his senior debut five days earlier and could have scored twice, being denied by a brilliant save by Petrovic in extra-time as his powerful header for Van Dijk's nod across goal was spectacularly tipped over the bar by the Serbian.

Liverpool's starting eleven had featured just three players who lined-up in their last major final, the Champions League showpiece in Paris two years ago.

Injuries of course played their part in that statistic with 11 players ruled out, including three influential members of the Reds' leadership group: vice-captain Trent Alexander-Arnold, Alisson Becker and Mohamed Salah.

There were also just four players who had started the 2022 Carabao Cup final against Thomas Tuchel's Chelsea, the additional starter being goalkeeper Caoimhin Kelleher.

The Irishman was Liverpool's hero that afternoon, scoring what proved to be the winning kick of the shoot-out.

He is far less of an unknown quantity these days and Liverpool are fortunate to have both he and Alisson among their squad.

He was one of the Reds heroes again this time around, proving that lightning can indeed strike twice with another key contribution. Indeed when the final whistle shrilled, the Liverpool players made a beeline for their no62.

Kelleher made nine saves in total during the game, including three vital interventions.

The first, after 20 minutes, was arguably the best, as he produced a point-blank save to deny a fiercely struck attempt by Palmer, Chelsea's best player, before the excellent Endo put his body on the line to block the follow-up and thwart Jackson.

With 85 minutes on the clock, Palmer released Gallagher in space on the left and he looked a certain scorer only for Kelleher to advance towards him and repel his attempt.

Then in the fourth of six added minutes at the end of normal time, the Blues had three attempts in the space of 10 seconds with Konate denying sub Christopher Nkunku before Palmer's effort from the rebound was blocked by Kelleher. Right-back Malo Gusto then fired the ball into the danger zone and, after the ball found its way back to Nkunku, Liverpool's keeper was there to gather again.

"I had a lot of family and friends who came across from Ireland so there was a whole crew here," he explained. "It's a nice moment for them. They've helped me a lot during my career, so it's a nice thing for them to come over to Wembley and experience a final as well. It was a proud moment for them and great that we could win again."

And so, in a mirror of the Reds' last League Cup triumph under Bob Paisley in 1983, Van Dijk insisted that the boss help him hoist the League Cup aloft - the first trophy of Klopp's remastered Liverpool 2.0.

The club's love affair with the tournament was a slow burner. It was 20 years after they first entered the competition before the Reds first lifted the silverware. Indeed in 1963/64 Liverpool were one of 10 of the 92 clubs who chose not to enter.

But the Liverpool of 2023/24 would not take a backward step.

Forget average age, forget big name opponents.

"Liverpool is a club made for major trophies," said assistant manager Pep Lijnders in his pre-match press conference. "Each year we should fight for them and that's what we'll try to do. We'll go for it."

And go for it they did.

Klopp began his long goodbye by claiming his eighth piece of silverware as Liverpool manager, exactly three months before his reign could end with a potential Europa League final in Dublin.

He stated afterwards that this was the most special of all his triumphs as a manager. It was a sentiment echoed by hundreds of thousands of Reds around the globe, all beaming with pride at what this young squad had achieved.

After all, we are Liverpool and this does mean more. And like those youngsters given their chance to shine beneath Wembley's giant arch, we're so glad that Jürgen is a red.

CHELSEA	STATS	LIVERPOOL
46	POSSESSION (%)	54
18	SHOTS	24
9	SHOTS ON TARGET	11
6	CORNERS	5
2	OFFSIDES	2

DOES IT ALMOST FEEL LIKE YOU'VE BEEN HERE BEFORE?

BY CHRIS McLOUGHLIN

But if you close your eyes, does it almost feel like nothing changed at all? And if you close your eyes, does it almost feel like you've been here before?

It was the same, but different. Liverpool v Chelsea at Wembley. 0-0 after 90 minutes. Woodwork struck. Chances missed. Goalkeepers doing their bits. The nerve-jangling prospect of penalties imminent. Again. But then Bobby Clark won a corner.

Bobby Clark, a recently turned 19-year-old whose previous eight first-team appearances had totalled 120 minutes, playing in a major cup final for Liverpool. And he wasn't even the least experienced player.

He won a corner via a deflected shot in the 118th minute and as Kostas Tsimikas jogged over to take it he rallied the travelling Kop, gesticulating for them to up the decibel levels.

The Reds, behind the goal in Wembley's East End – having been in the West End for all three visits in 2022 – responded. They'd already been magnificent. *Allez Allez Allez* had rung out incessantly in the first period of extra-time as Liverpool played towards the Chelsea fans. Now it was time to suck the ball into the net.

Tsimikas placed the ball in the corner quadrant and puffed out his cheeks. He looked up and struck it with his left foot towards the near post.

Mykhailo Mudryk jumped. He was the first man. It was his corner to head clear. But arriving behind him at pace, like a thoroughbred timing his gallop perfectly to snatch victory on the line at Aintree, was Virgil van Dijk.

He soared through the air, met the ball with his head and

glanced a header goalwards with laser precision. Djordje Petrovic, the Chelsea goalkeeper, took a step to his left. In that split second his body weight was going in the wrong direction.

Petrovic adjusted and dived to his right, but he might as well have waved the ball goodbye with a handkerchief. The net rippled. The travelling Kop, on their toes for 118 minutes, soared like their skipper, limbs moving in every direction.

Virgil ran to the corner flag and collapsed to the turf on his back. Tsimikas grabbed his legs like a WWE wrestler eyeing up a Boston crab, James McConnell dived on top of him.

James McConnell, a not-so-recently turned 19-year-old whose previous six first-team appearances had totalled 97 minutes,

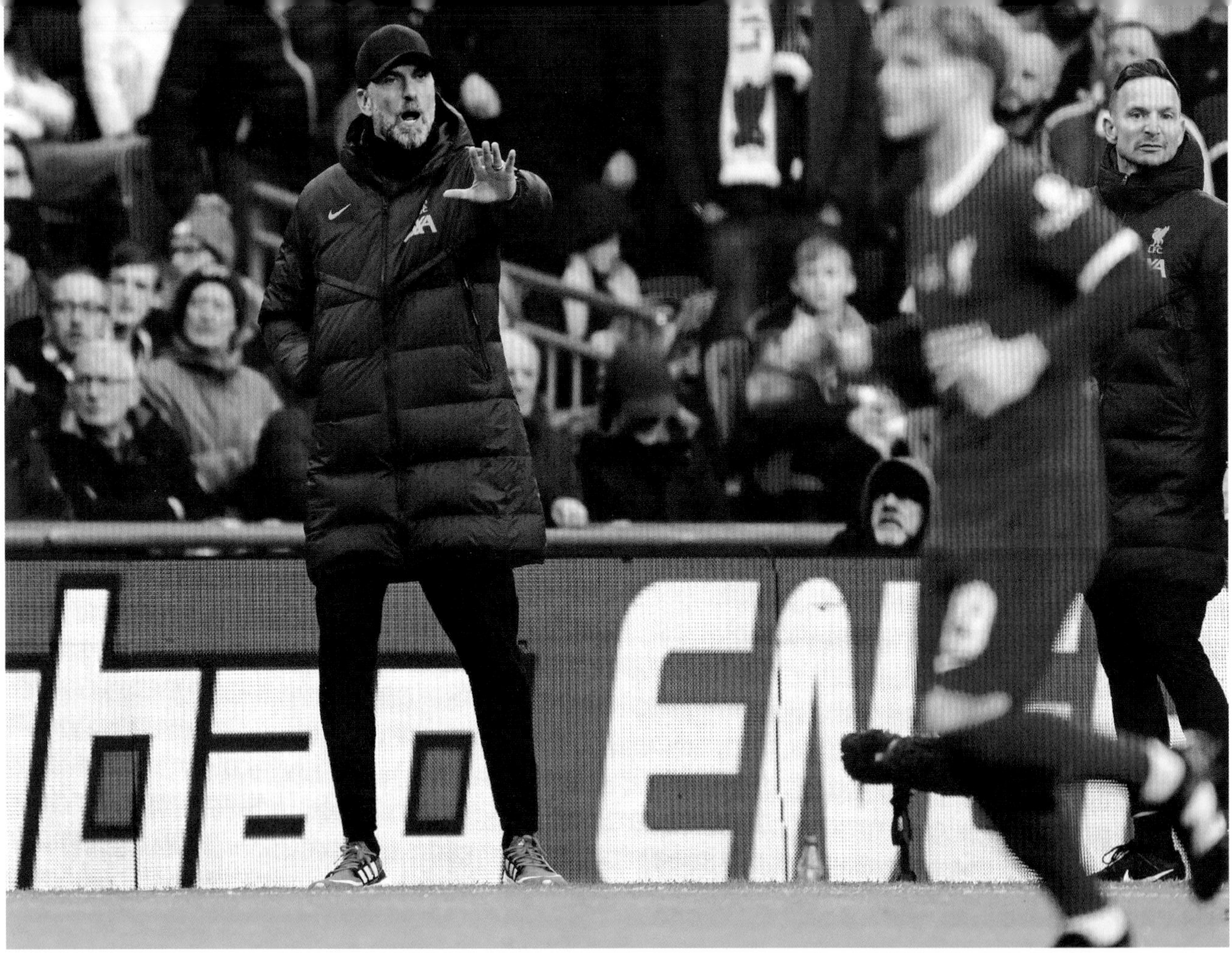

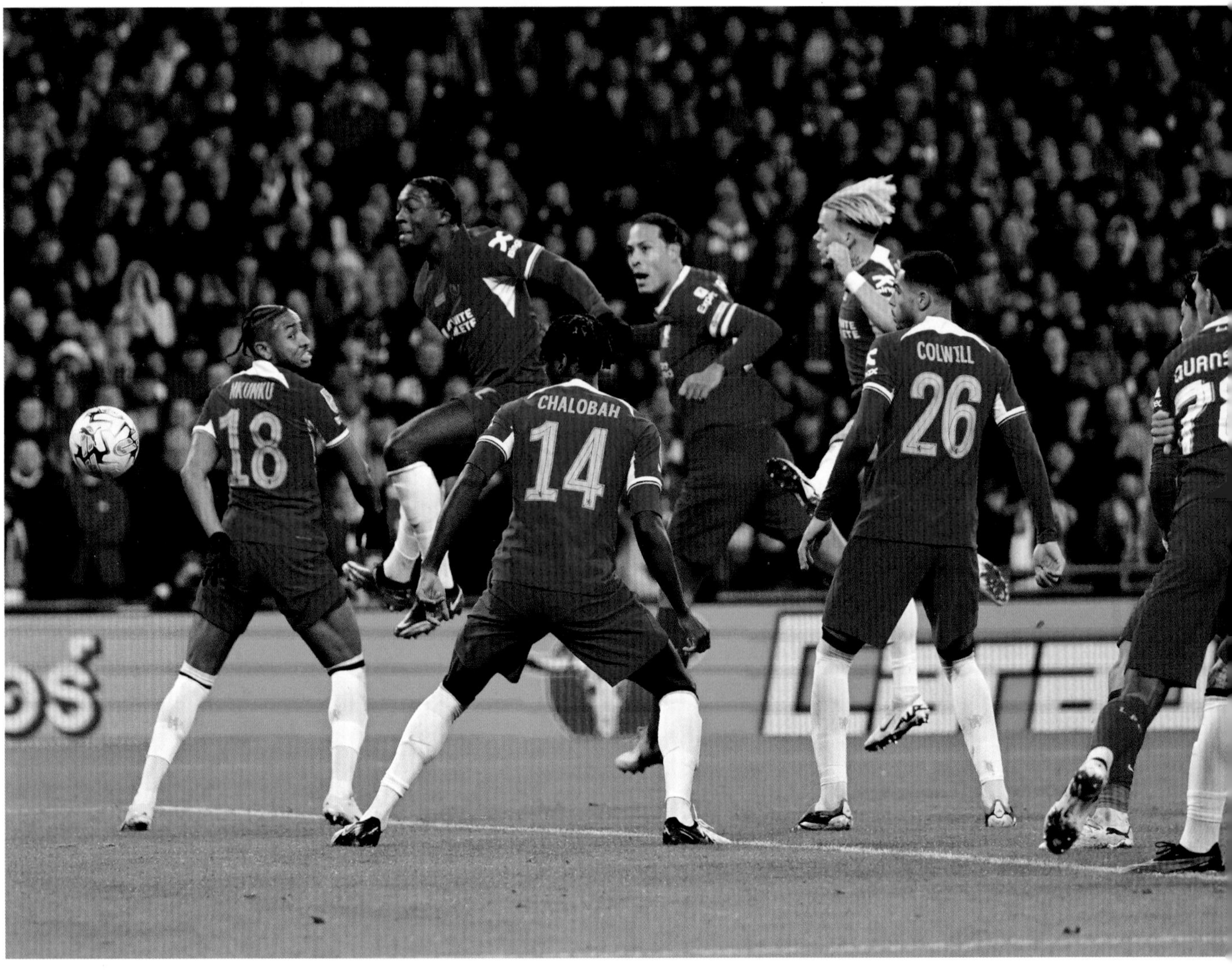
NKUNKU
18
CHALOBAH
14
COLWILL
26

playing in a major cup final for Liverpool. And he wasn't even the least experienced player.

On the Liverpool bench, Darwin Nunez sprinted down the Wembley steps, bounded over a gate and advertising hoarding like a gazelle running free in the savannas of Africa and celebrated pitchside. Dominik Szoboszlai wasn't far behind him and Curtis Jones hobbled down the steps after them. Adrenaline can do magical things to injuries, but don't ever doubt what it means to players who aren't playing. The team spirit Jürgen Klopp has built underpins afternoons like this. We are all Liverpool. This means more. This means everything.

The Reds were 1-0 up. And if you close your eyes, does it almost feel like you've been here before? We had, about an hour earlier.

Virgil won the game in normal time. At least he thought he had. There were 60 minutes on the clock when he soared to meet Andy Robertson's free-kick and head it past Petrovic. He celebrated in the same corner of Wembley as the sky turned red, yet the dream stealer was lying in wait.

VAR official John Brooks sent referee Chris Kavanagh to the pitchside monitor to check for offside. Not against van Dijk, who was a country mile on, but against Wataru Endo, who was on the edge of the box and involved in a clash with Levi Colwill.

It seemed innocuous. The kind of coming together that was brushed off as 'mutual holding' when Diogo Jota was rugby tackled to the turf at Brentford eight days earlier, but Kavanagh returned to the pitch drawing an imaginary rectangle above his head and van Dijk was denied his moment of glory. For now.

The travelling Kop, who had turned the railways and motorways down to the capital red, were not to be denied. Virgil's winning goal in extra-time made those 6am alarm calls – for those who had a lie-in – worthwhile. WE WIN CUPS read one of the many banners in the Liverpool end. It told no lies.

You'll Never Walk Alone sounded magnificent in the moments before kick-off. Scarves aloft, hearts on sleeves, the Anfield anthem filling Southern skies. The Chelsea fans waved their plastic flags and went *One Step Beyond* with a bit of Suggs. It was soon drowned out by Jamie Webster's version of *Allez Allez Allez*. Wembley was loud. It felt like a cup final.

Giant v-shaped banners featuring players from both sides were unfurled on the pitch. The Liverpool one had van Dijk, Darwin Nunez, Dominik Szoboszlai and Trent Alexander-Arnold upon it. But only the skipper was fit to play, and with Mo Salah, Alisson, Jota, Joel Matip, Thiago, Curtis Jones, Stefan Bajcetic and Ben Doak joining them on the injury list, the Reds fielded three players aged 21 and under – Ryan Gravenberch, Harvey Elliott and Conor Bradley – for the first time in a major cup final in the club's history.

The bench was so young that it felt like Adrian, Joe Gomez and Tsimikas were overseeing a school trip. But Klopp's Carabao Cup kids would have their part to play.

After shaking hands with each other and exchanging pre-match pleasantries with the dignataries, both sides got into huddles and Ibrahima Konate got proceedings underway by finding touch after Alexis Mac Allister rolled the ball back to him.

Wembley was a picture. Red v Blue always looks striking and Liverpool v Chelsea is the most played domestic cup final in English football history. Klopp's boys looked about seven feet tall in all-red while the reflective club crest on Chelsea's all-blue strips made it look like a flickering satellite TV box standby button was upon their chests as they ran.

The West Londoners' followers sang about Steven Gerrard.

The travelling Kop questioned Chelsea's history. When *Fields of Anfield Road* rang out about 16 minutes in you could have heard it in Athenry. Tragedy chanting has no place in football, so to hear such a thing from a section of Chelsea fans as Gravenberch lay prone on the turf, awaiting a stretcher after an unpunished late tackle from Moises Caicedo, did the majority of their support a disservice.

Caoimhin Kelleher's world-class save from Cole Palmer, Raheem Sterling's disallowed goal for offside, Cody Gakpo's header against the bar and Ben Chilwell and Bradley getting booked for a scuffle were the highlights of the usual rollercoaster before half-time. For Bradley to be moved upfront after Gravenberch's injury, Joe Gomez coming on at right-back, only highlighted Liverpool's injury crisis further.

At half-time, the big screens showed Liverpool fan Ruby being beaten 3-1 by Chelsea fan Zak in a game of EA Sports FC 24. It was Chelsea's first 3-1 win against the Reds since 2009, but wouldn't be repeated on the pitch.

After Virgil's 60th minute header was controversially disallowed, Conor Gallagher hit the post and was denied in a one-v-one by another outstanding Kelleher save. If ever there was an endorsement of how good Alisson is, it is how good Kelleher is. At 99% of other clubs, he starts every game.

As extra-time loomed, Klopp turned to his bench. Robertson, Mac Allister and Gakpo were withdrawn, Tsimikas, McConnell and Jayden Danns came on. Jayden Danns, a recently turned 18-year-old whose previous sole first-team appearances had totalled two minutes, playing in a major cup final for Liverpool. And he was the least experienced player, and also the second Red after Ian Rush to make his second appearance for LFC in a major cup final. He almost scored, too.

Kelleher had to diffuse a stoppage-time goalmouth scramble to take Liverpool v Chelsea to extra-time – again – and evoking memories of Istanbul the travelling Kop belted out *You'll Never Walk Alone* in the interval. Four minutes later, van Dijk headed Elliott's cross back across goal and Danns headed goalwards, but Petrovic pushed the ball onto the roof of the net. Fairy tale denied.

YNWA rang out again in the extra-time half-time interval and Klopp put his arm around Tsimikas as he gave the Greek Scouser instructions. Jarell Quansah was also sent on for Konate while Luis Diaz and Elliott both looked like they were carrying knocks.

The Chelsea fans found their voices again, singing *Three Little Birds* – the anthem of Liverpool's run to the 2016 Europa League final – and when Elliott's 116th-minute header was somehow kept out by Petrovic, who clutched the ball before Danns could bundle it over the line, they must have thought every little thing was gonna be alright. But they were wrong.

Two minutes later, Clark's shot was deflected over and Alan Hardaker Trophy-winning player-of-the-match van Dijk – but only just from Kelleher – leapt highest to head home the winner he had earlier been denied.

Scarves twirled in the Liverpool end as *Ring of Fire* rang out before *I Feel Fine* – the Klopp tribute tune that will undoubtedly provide the soundtrack to the end of his time as manager – echoed around Wembley. And when the full-time whistle blew, it was Kelleher the players all rushed towards. He'd kept another cup final clean sheet against Chelsea and this time didn't even have to take a penalty to win it.

As the celebrations continued, *Fields of Anfield Road* got another airing, Klopp gave his traditional three fist pumps with more gusto than Chelsea's right-back, and the Virgil van Dijk song was belted out as he walked towards the Liverpool end after doing a post-match TV interview.

And it was the big Dutchman who led the Reds up the Wembley steps, received his medal and player-of-the-match award from the EFL's ex-Reds CEO Rick Parry and then shouted to his manager – who had Kelleher in a bear-hug – 'together'.

In echoes of 1983, when the retiring Bob Paisley was invited to lift the League Cup by skipper Graeme Souness, Klopp hoisted the three-handled trophy aloft with Virgil and then

bounced around like it was the first piece of silverware he'd ever grasped. Bastille's *Pompeii* blasted out over the PA system, ticker-tape flew through the air, the cup was passed along the line to player-by-player cheers from Liverpool fans and back at Anfield the Champions Wall needed yet another update.

The players returned to the pitch to lift the cup again by the green Carabao Cup podium before lining up in front of their loyal supporters for a moving, communal singing of *You'll Never Walk Alone*. Elliott, a lifelong supporter, held aloft a scarf and Klopp broke ranks before the song had ended before darting back into the line between Pep Lijnders and Vitor Matos. Then it was time for Dua Lipa.

Even Gravenberch, who like the outstanding Endo left Wembley on crutches and wearing a protective boot, bounced around on one leg as *One Kiss* got the party started. Again.

Three Little Birds was reclaimed shortly afterwards and the 11 players at Wembley who had come through the Academy – or been signed at young age – lined up for the photo of the day with the injured Alexander-Arnold, Bajcetic and Ben Doak joining Quansah, Danns, Clark, McConnell, Lewis Koumas, Trey Nyoni, Bradley and Elliott. Somebody get Alex Inglethorpe a medal too.

When the players finally left the pitch, a beaming Sir Kenny Dalglish – who had been sat next to his old strike partner Rush in the stands – was in the tunnel waiting to congratulate them.

The party continued in the dressing room as Diaz, who ran himself to a standstill, danced around with a Colombian flag wrapped around his waist like a skirt and the Carabao Cup playing the part of his dance partner. It's a 10 from Len, as they used to say on *Strictly Come Dancing*.

Later that night, on the flight home to Liverpool, a sleeping Klopp was photographed cradling the League Cup like it was a precious grandchild.

And when he closed his eyes, it almost felt like he'd been here before.

THERE ARE PLACES I REMEMBER...

As always, Liverpool fans ventured to Wembley in their thousands, hoping to watch their heroes win and those dreams came true again in spectacular fashion...

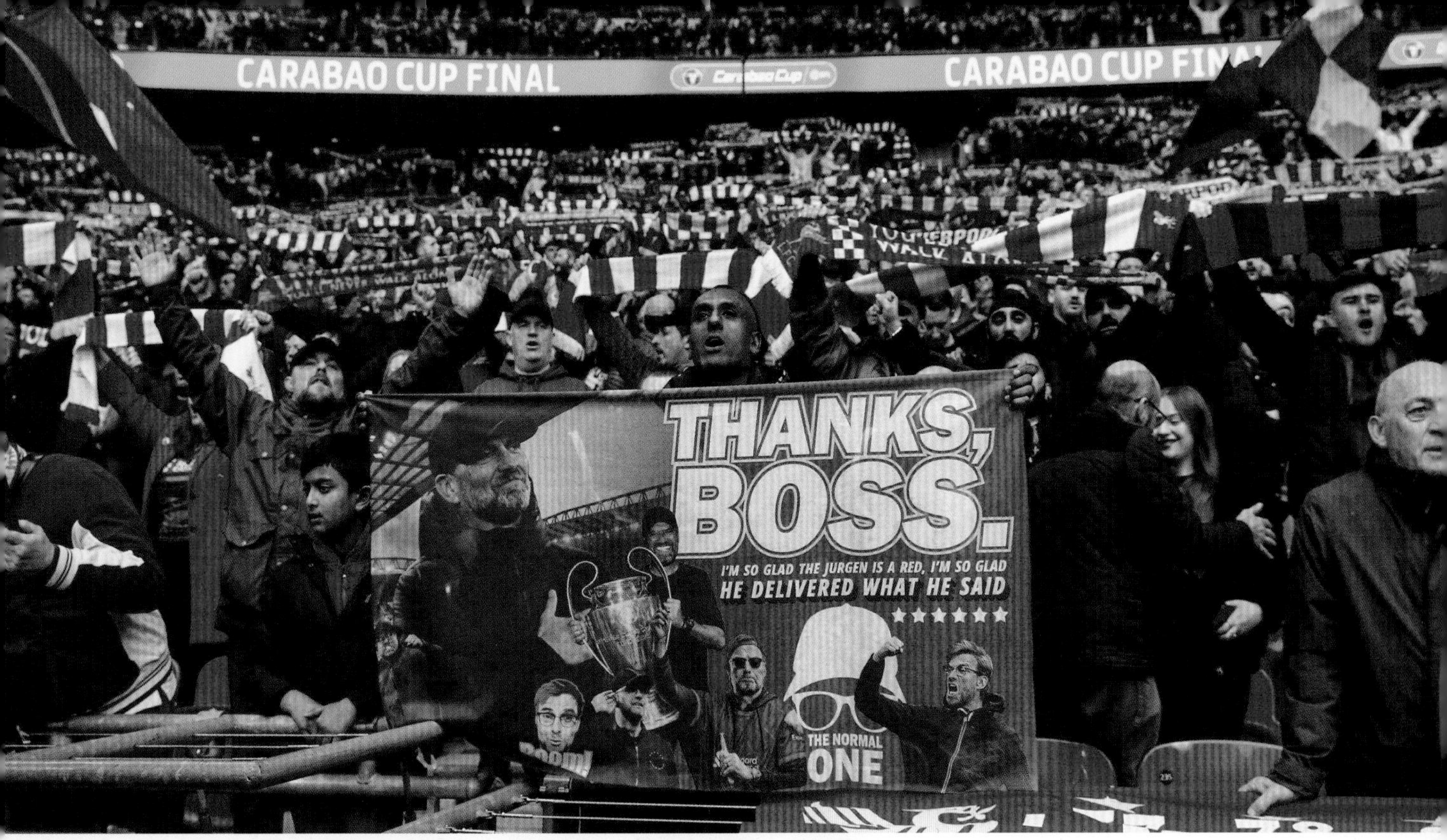

CARABAO CUP FINAL
CARABAO CUP FINAL
THANKS, BOSS.
I'M SO GLAD THE JURGEN IS A RED, I'M SO GLAD
HE DELIVERED WHAT HE SAID
THE NORMAL
ONE

LIVERPOOL
LIVERPOOL FC

WELCOME TO THE
KLOPP REVOLUTION
JÜRGEN
KLOPP
LIVERPOOL
MANAGER

SZOBOSZLAI STUNNER STEALS THE SHOW

LIVERPOOL 3
LEICESTER CITY 1

Goals: McAteer (3), Gakpo (48), Szoboszlai (70), Jota (89).
27.09.23 • Anfield • Attendance: 49,732
Referee: Tim Robinson

LIVERPOOL (4-3-3): Kelleher, Jones (C) (Bajcetic 79), Konate, Quansah, Tsimikas (Chambers 90), Elliott, Endo, Gravenberch (Nunez 65), Doak (Szoboszlai 65), Gakpo, Jota.
Subs not used: Adrian, Van Dijk, Diaz, Mac Allister, Matip.
Booked: Endo.

LEICESTER CITY (4-3-3): Stolarczyk, Pereira (C), Souttar, Coady, Justin, Akgun (Dewsbury-Hall 65), Choudhury, Casadei (Ndidi 57), Albrighton (Fatawu 64), Iheanacho (Daka 64), McAteer.
Subs not used: Hermansen, Faes, Winks, Mavididi, Vestergaard.
Booked: Pereira, Choudhury.

PRESS BOX: JAMES PEARCE, THE ATHLETIC
"Wataru Endo completed 47 of his 52 passes (90 per cent) and retrieved possession on 13 occasions, more than any other Liverpool player. He also made four interceptions and won three of his four aerial duels. On a night packed full of positives for Klopp, the brilliance of Szoboszlai stole the show, but the sight of Endo stamping his authority on the game bodes well for the challenges ahead."

PUNDIT: PHIL THOMPSON, LFCTV
"Szoboszlai's goal was absolutely incredible. To strike it the way he did was truly exceptional. He just absolutely caught it and it flew in. Honestly, it was dangerous because if that net wasn't there it could have hurt somebody! I don't know why the 'keeper dived, he was nowhere near it. It was just like Stevie G."

REPORT:

On another night Liverpool supporters would have left Anfield talking about Diogo Jota's backheel goal, Ben Doak's first start in a home game or Conor Coady making two goalline clearances. Not tonight.

The only name on the lips of every Red was Dominik Szoboszlai after he scored with a Kop-end howitzer that thumped the underside of the crossbar on the way in.

Szoboszlai had only been on the pitch for five minutes when he received a pass from Wataru Endo and struck the ball from 25 yards out like Jan Molby or Steven Gerrard in their pomp. Foxes goalkeeper Jakub Stolarczyk dived, but wouldn't have gotten near it had he been wearing giant foam gloves.

It was an exceptional hit from the 22-year-old Hungarian international skipper to finally give much-changed Liverpool a lead they completely deserved and, ultimately, a place in the fourth round.

Jürgen Klopp made 10 changes from the side that had beaten West Ham 3-1 to go second in the Premier League table three days earlier, with Curtis Jones the only player retaining his place, but not his position.

With Trent Alexander-Arnold, Joe Gomez and Conor Bradley all sidelined, Jones deputised at right-back and also wore the captain's armband for the second time in his Liverpool career. His win record is 100 per cent.

Endo, Ryan Gravenberch, Jarell Quansah and Doak all made their first starts at Anfield, while it would also be a proud night for Caoimhin Kelleher - who finished the game wearing the skipper's armband for the first time - and Academy left-back Luke Chambers, brought on for his LFC debut.

→

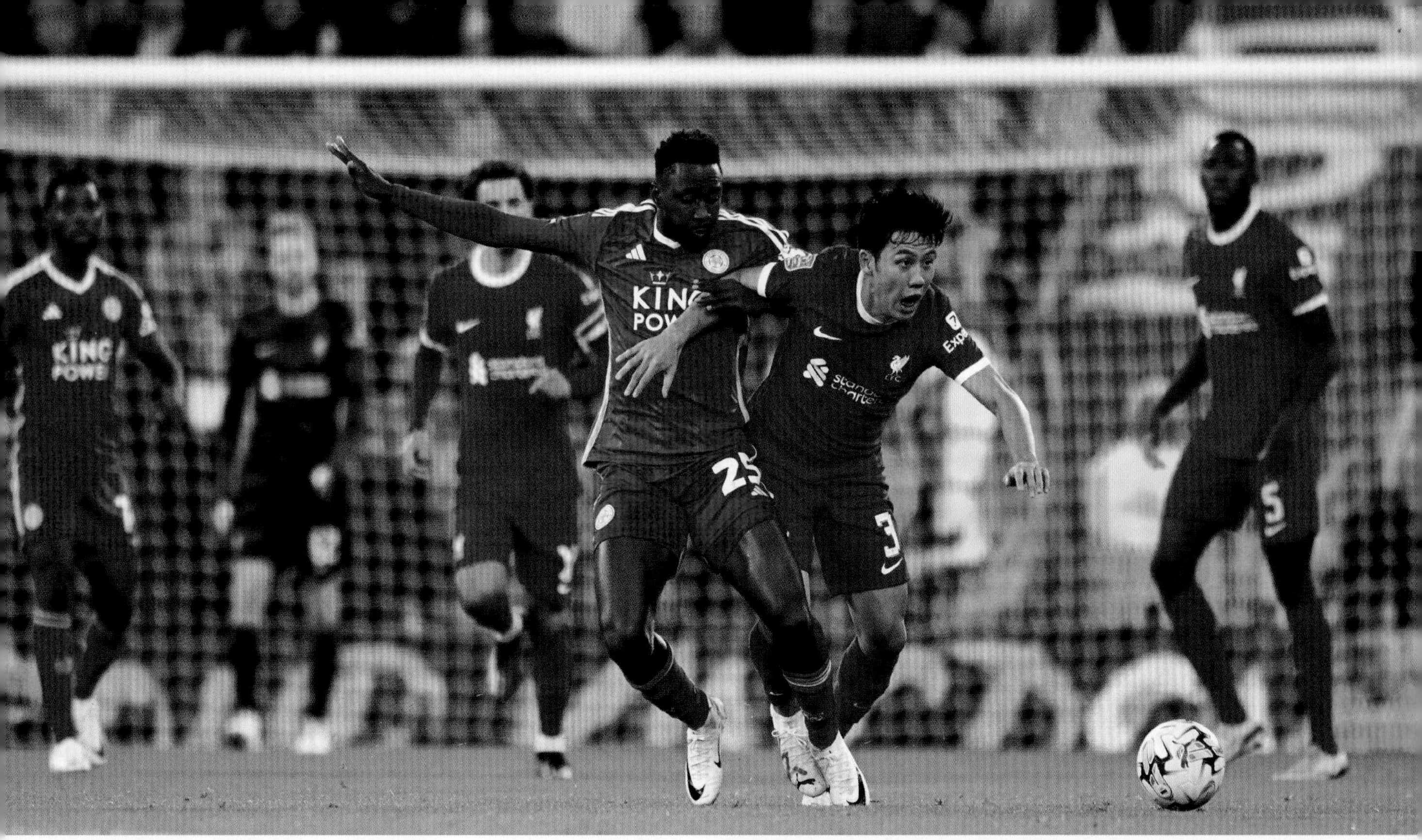
KING POWER

KING POWER
Expedia

DOAK
GAKPO
18

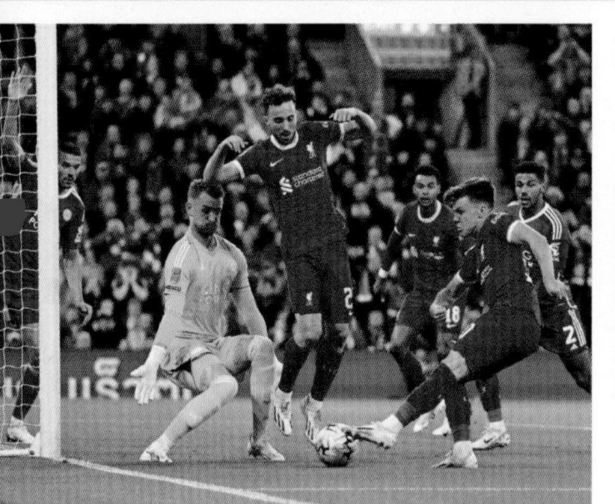

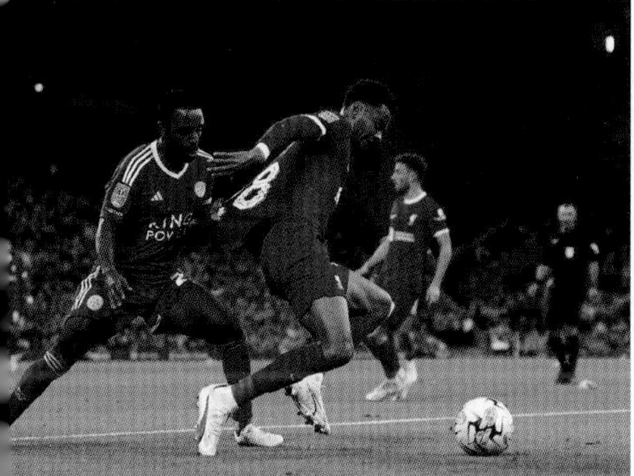

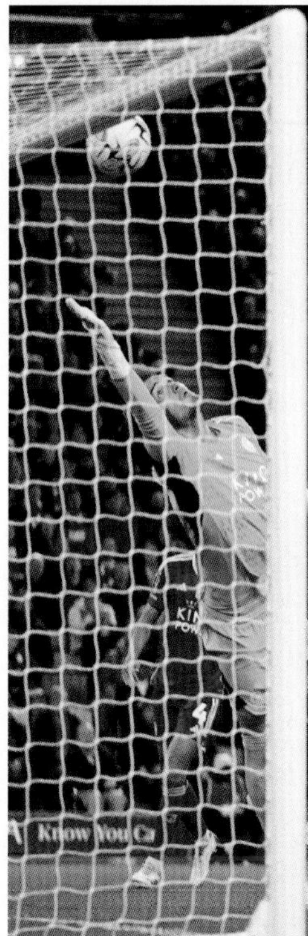

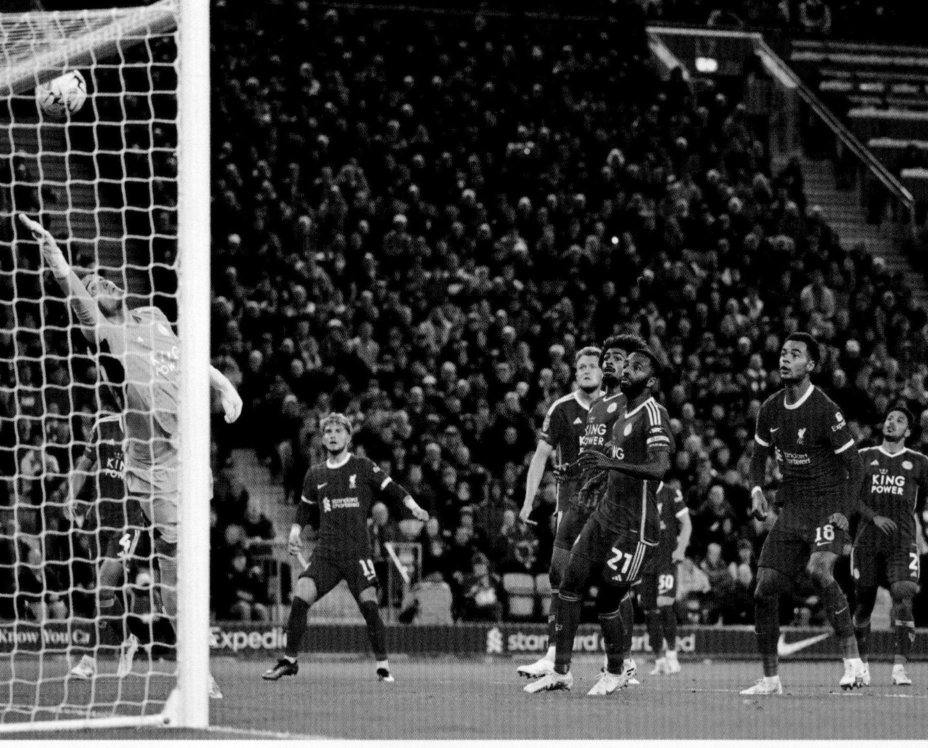

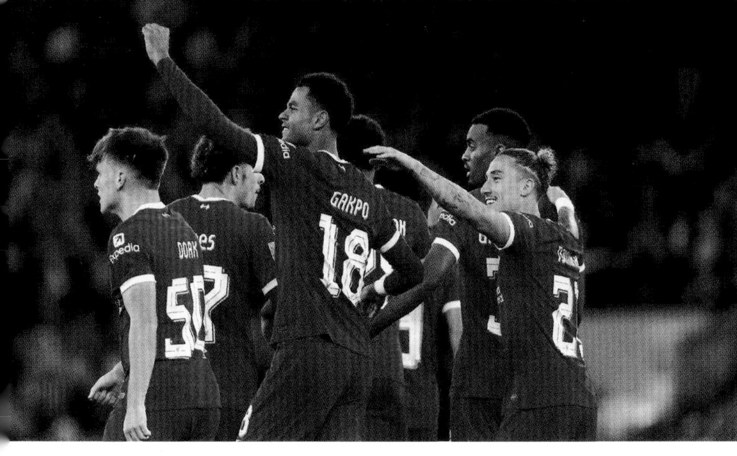

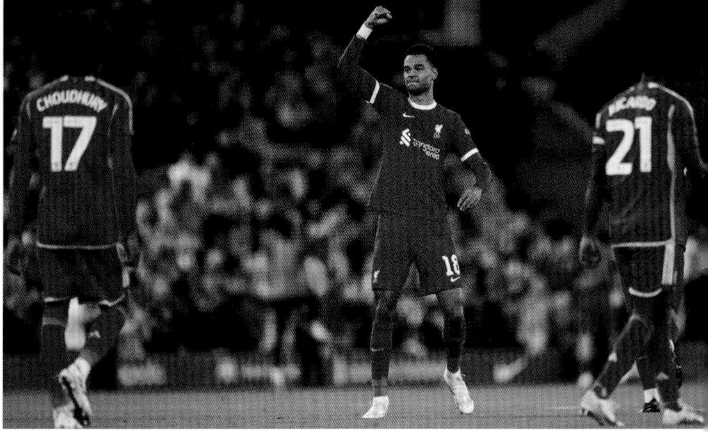

CHOUDHURY
17
21

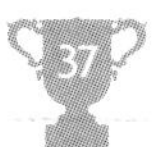

An unpunished foul on the man he replaced, Kostas Tsimikas, led to Enzo Maresca's Leicester taking the lead. The Championship leaders took advantage of Tsimikas being left on the turf after having his Achilles tendon clipped and Kasey McAteer was sent clear to beat Kelleher in a one-v-one.

It proved to be the Foxes' only shot on target all night whereas the Reds created 20 chances and should have been at least level by half-time.

Diogo Jota seemed certain to score from Harvey Elliott's cross, but the ball went between his legs instead of into the net. When Quansah had a shot parried, Doak pounced on the rebound, but blasted against the underside of the crossbar.

Cody Gakpo then beat Stolarczyk with a header from a Tsimikas free-kick, but ex-Red Conor Coady - who was reminded by the Kop that he spent last season on loan at Everton - cleared off the line on his Leicester debut.

An equaliser finally arrived three minutes after the break. Endo intercepted a pass, Gravenberch dropped his shoulder to beat Hamza Choudhury and slipped a pass to Gakpo, who struck a low shot on the turn into the bottom corner.

It was almost a Dutch double when Gakpo headed Elliott's chipped cross over Stolarczyk, but the ball struck the crossbar again before being cleared off the goalline by Marc Albrighton.

Darwin Nunez and Szoboszlai were sent on in the 65th minute and five minutes later Liverpool's number eight struck with perhaps the most thunderous goal seen at Anfield since Mo Salah's rocket against Chelsea in 2019.

He would try his luck again shortly afterwards, this time from a Nunez pass, but the ball flashed over. Klopp later described it as "another grenade."

Nunez had his own opportunity to make it 3-1 only to place a shot from a stunning pass by Stefan Bajcetic - on for Jones at right-back with Kelleher taking over as skipper - narrowly wide of the upright.

Quansah and Ibrahima Konate both made timely interventions to snuff out a couple of Leicester half-chances and it was the 20-year-old centre-back who created Liverpool's third in the 89th minute.

Up for a corner that was cleared but retrieved by Elliott, Quansah beat James Justin on the right, glided into the box and squared the ball for Jota to guide it home with a gloriously deft backheel flick. There was still time for Coady to block another goalbound effort from Elliott and left-back Chambers to come on for a stoppage-time debut, but Leicester were now well beaten.

On any other night Kopites would have left Anfield talking about Jota's improvised finish and a fourth consecutive 3-1 comeback victory having conceded first each time, but when you've seen a shot fly in like the exocet missile Dominik Szoboszlai hit, why think about anything else?

LIVERPOOL	STATS	LEICESTER CITY
57	POSSESSION (%)	43
29	SHOTS	4
10	SHOTS ON TARGET	1
10	CORNERS	2
1	OFFSIDES	2

MANAGER: JÜRGEN KLOPP

"Minute by minute, we grew into that game and it was a top performance, to be honest. We kept going and improved during the game as a team clearly, but individually as well a lot of performances stepped up. Super signs tonight, I really like that a lot. The boys enjoyed playing in it and you saw how they were pressing until the last second. They really enjoyed it and that's cool."

FOR THE RECORD:

Ryan Gravenberch became the first player to get assists in his first two starts for Liverpool since Jordon Ibe in 2013.

ALSO THIS ROUND:

Newcastle United 1-0 Manchester City
Exeter City 1-0 Luton Town
Brentford 0-1 Arsenal

BOURNEMOUTH 1
LIVERPOOL 2

Goals: Gakpo (31), Kluivert (64), Nunez (70).
01.11.23 • Vitality Stadium •
Attendance: 11,116 • Referee: John Brooks

BOURNEMOUTH (4-2-3-1): Radu, Smith (C) (Aarons 82), Mepham, Zabarnyi, Kerkez, Scott (Moore 81), Billing (Tavernier 61), Semenyo (Brooks 74), Christie, Kluivert (Traore 74), Solanke.
Subs not used: Plain, Rothwell, Ouattara, Senesi. Booked: Kerkez, Scott.

LIVERPOOL (4-3-3): Kelleher, Gomez, Matip, Quansah, Tsimikas, Elliott (Nunez 60), Endo (Alexander-Arnold 61), Jones (Mac Allister 61), Szoboszlai (Gravenberch 76), Salah (C), Gakpo (Jota 81).
Subs not used: Adrian, van Dijk, Konate, Scanlon. Booked: Gakpo.

PRESS BOX: JEREMEY WILSON, DAILY TELEGRAPH
"From the eye of the storm came a winner that, even in any weather conditions, could be fairly described as a winner from the gods. Step forward Darwin Nunez who proved himself impervious to lashing sideways rain and genuinely galeforce winds on the Dorset coast to deliver a wonderful curling finish into the top corner. Nunez had only been on the pitch for 10 minutes when he produced his breathtaking intervention."

PUNDIT: GEMMA BONNER, LFCTV
"When Nunez came on you could see he wanted to do something almost straight away. They gave him too much space. He's so direct, he always wants to cut in from the left and we've seen how well he can hit the ball. It was a great finish."

STORM DARWIN

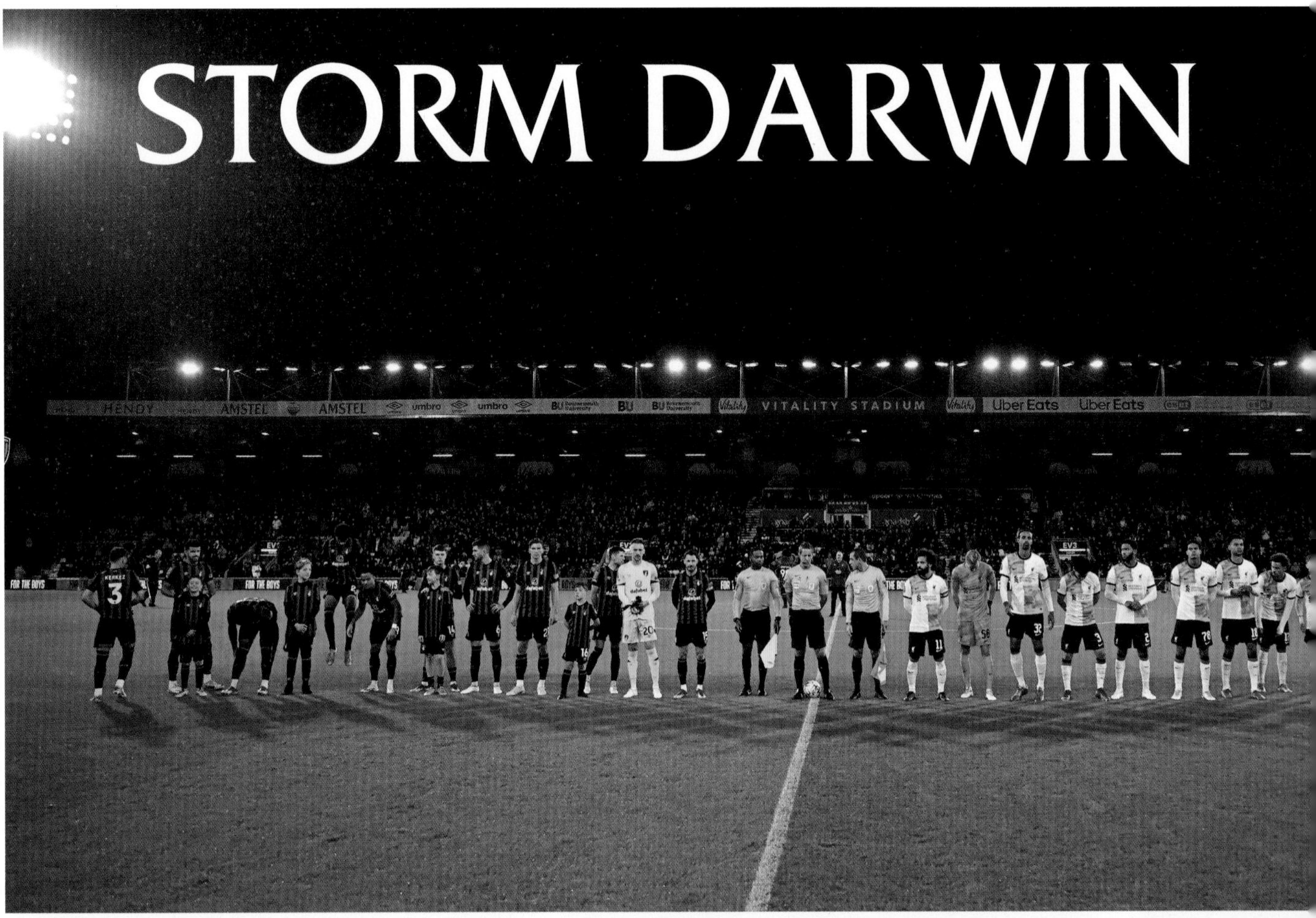

MANAGER: JÜRGEN KLOPP
"It's all about winning, it's all about getting through. It was really difficult for both teams. First half we could have scored more goals, we didn't. Second half obviously we realised it would have been a good idea to have scored more goals because the wind changed the game again. We scored our second goal, a wonderful goal, and then we fought extremely hard. We had good moments but it is all about attitude in these moments. It was a top cup game in strange, strange circumstances."

FOR THE RECORD:
Mo Salah became the third African player to captain Liverpool from the start of a game after Arthur Riley and Kolo Toure.

ALSO THIS ROUND:
Manchester United 0-3 Newcastle United
West Ham United 3-1 Arsenal
Chelsea 2-0 Blackburn Rovers

REPORT:

The World Meteorological Organisation names storms alphabetically on a six-year cycle. Storm Agnes and Storm Babet had already caused havoc in the UK in September and October, now Liverpool were welcomed to the South Coast for this Carabao Cup fourth round tie by Storm Ciaran.

Perhaps plans to name the next one Storm Debi should be ditched following events at the Vitality Stadium, however. Storm Darwin would be more appropriate as Darwin Nunez's brilliant winning goal certainly went down a storm with the travelling Kop.

Driving rain and gale force winds made the second half of this clash a test of physicality and attitude above all else, but it was a touch of class that settled it.

Yet Nunez's winner was another goal that again epitomised the intoxicating combination of rawness,

Strategic
DARWIN
9

AARONS
37
9

GAKPO
18
9

dafabet

STATS		
BOURNEMOUTH		LIVERPOOL
33	POSSESSION (%)	67
16	SHOTS	18
7	SHOTS ON TARGET	7
5	CORNERS	7
3	OFFSIDES	2

belief and quality that has made the Uruguayan frontman such a fan favourite.

He causes chaos and while you're never quite sure what the end product is going to be with Nunez, his goal here was up there in quality with his double in the 2-1 Premier League win at Newcastle earlier in the season. And just like at St James' Park, Darwin did the damage after coming on from the bench.

There were 70 minutes on the clock when Trent Alexander-Arnold, on as a substitute in midfield, sprayed a diagonal pass out to Nunez on the left. He miscontrolled it, sparking ironic jeers from the Bournemouth fans.

But as the travelling Kopites in the stand behind Darwin responded with shouts of 'Nunez, Nunez', Liverpool's number nine cut back inside from a wide position and unleashed a beautiful, curling shot that dipped over Andrei Radu and underneath the crossbar.

It was a stunning strike, reminiscent of one Luis Suarez scored in a League Cup win at Stoke City back in 2011/12, and high in technique as Nunez was shooting into the wind.

The ongoing chants of 'Nunez, Nunez' were so loud when the Uruguayan ran to the travelling Kop that the wind probably carried the noise all the way to Bournemouth Pier, not that anyone in their right mind would be anywhere near the sea on such a filthy night.

Nunez's winning goal was no more than Liverpool deserved. Jürgen Klopp's men created plenty of opportunities to have stormed to victory before the break, but ended up battling the elements as much as Bournemouth in the second period.

The ongoing absence of Luis Diaz on compassionate leave following the kidnapping of his father in Colombia meant that Dominik Szoboszlai pushed forward into the front three with Cody Gakpo on the left and Mo Salah - skippering Liverpool for the first time - operating through the centre.

Caoimhin Kelleher had to make a smart save to foil Justin Kluivert in the 13th minute, but the best opportunity in the opening half-hour fell to Harvey Elliott, who could only sidefoot straight at Radu from Szoboszlai's pull-back.

Szoboszlai himself had an effort deflected wide by Cherries captain Adam Smith before the breakthrough came from the corner. Kostas Tsimikas's outswinger was cleared as far as Elliott on the edge of the box and his low effort was redirected goalwards by Gakpo. Radu saved, but the Dutchman pounced on the rebound. 1-0 Liverpool.

Five minutes later, Szoboszlai fired a daisy-cutter narrowly wide of Radu's post and 15 minutes after the break Salah met a lovely Elliott cross with his head, but also angled the ball wide. Moments later Bournemouth sprung into life and Antoine Semenyo sliced a gilt-edged chance to level as Jarell Quansah - outstanding enough at centre-back to be named as player-of-the-match in just his fourth first-team start - slid in to challenge while Kelleher needed to use both hands to push a 25-yard shot from Marcus Tavernier over the crossbar.

With the wind now blowing directly into Liverpool faces, defending set-pieces became trickier than putting a deckchair up on the beach. Alex Scott had already sent in a corner that looped over Kelleher, forcing Joe Gomez to head off the goalline, and it was from a similar corner that Bournemouth equalised.

Again Scott's corner caught on the wind and went over the Liverpool goalkeeper, but this time Kluivert was lurking at the back post to head in.

It gave the hosts a chance of taking the game to penalties or even nicking a winner, but Storm Darwin blew those hopes away in the 70th minute to send the Reds into the Carabao Cup quarter-final.

JONES AT THE DOUBLE

LIVERPOOL 5 WEST HAM UNITED 1

Goals: Szoboszlai (28), Jones (56, 84), Gakpo (71), Bowen (77), Salah (82).

20.12.23 • Anfield • Attendance: 57,332

Referee: Tim Robinson

LIVERPOOL (4-3-3): Kelleher, Gomez, Quansah, van Dijk (C) (Konate 60), Tsimikas (Bradley 69), Szoboszlai (Salah 60), Endo (Alexander-Arnold 60), Jones, Elliott, Gakpo (Diaz 78), Nunez. Subs not used: Adrian, Clark, Gordon, McConnell. Booked: Nunez.

WEST HAM UNITED (4-2-3-1): Areola, Coufal (Kehrer 72), Mavropanos, Ogbonna (C), Johnson, Soucek, Alvarez (Ings 81), Kudus (Ward-Prowse 72), Fornals, Benrahma (Paqueta 57), Bowen. Subs not used: Fabianski, Cresswell, Zouma, Emerson, Mubama. Booked: Alvarez.

PRESS BOX: RICHARD JOLLY, THE INDEPENDENT

"After Liverpool spent Sunday accumulating shots without scoring, the floodgates opened in the Anfield rain. Their 34 efforts brought no goals against Manchester United. Three days later, they tried and tried and tried again and 29 attempts yielded five goals, each courtesy of a fine finish. Persistent, determined, enterprising and excellent, they demolished West Ham."

PUNDIT: HARRY REDKNAPP, SKY SPORTS

"Curtis Jones could walk into almost any team in the Premier League and play regularly. But he obviously wants to stay there, win his place at Liverpool and it looks to me it's only a matter of time before he gets that regular berth in the team. He looks too good not to play. He played with so much energy."

MANAGER: JÜRGEN KLOPP
"We were brave in our positioning, our second ball game was exceptional. It was a really, really good performance from start to finish. The boys enjoyed it a lot. They worked hard but enjoyed it too with joyful football in moments. It was one of those nights where you really could enjoy the game from start to finish because it was just a really good performance in all departments. It was difficult for West Ham, obviously, and we won the game. Everything is good."

FOR THE RECORD:
Curtis Jones' first goal was Liverpool's 500th in the League Cup - the first was scored by Tommy Leishmann against Luton at Anfield in 1960.

ALSO THIS ROUND:
Chelsea 1-1 Newcastle (Chelsea win 4-2 on pens)
Everton 1-1 Fulham (Fulham win 7-6 on pens)
Port Vale 0-3 Middlesbrough

REPORT:

You wait all your life to score in front of a packed Kop and then two goals come along at once. For Curtis Jones, Liverpool's 5-1 quarter-final win against West Ham at Anfield was the milestone night that should have happened sooner.

The Scouse midfielder's first Anfield goal was a winner against Everton in the FA Cup in January 2020. His most recent was the opener in a 4-3 Premier League success against Spurs in April 2023. Both special, both scored at the Anfield Road end.

He twice scored in front of the Kop in 2020 - clinching a 2-0 win against Aston Villa with Liverpool already crowned as Premier League champions and his first Champions League goal was the winner against Erik Ten Hag's Ajax - but Anfield was empty.

The coronavirus pandemic meant both games were played behind closed doors, so when Jones ran onto a Darwin Nunez pass in the 56th minute and squeezed a shot between the legs of Hammers goalie Alphonse Areola to make it 2-0, he finally got to experience the thrill of scoring in front of a full Kop.

'Curtis, Curtis Jones', they chanted, 'Curtis, Curtis Jones'.

The fact that it was also Jones who completed this comfortable victory by bringing an intelligent Trent Alexander-Arnold pass forward, slaloming his way into the West Ham box and smashing the ball into the Kop net was another plot twist.

→

His first goal was Liverpool's 500th in the League Cup and his second was his 13th goal on his 113th appearance against a side managed by David Moyes, who had previously lost 13 of his 20 visits to Anfield.

Moyes' 14th defeat was his heaviest yet and in truth the scoreline flattered West Ham. Areola saved six of the Reds' eleven shots on target, Nunez hit the post and Mo Salah missed a sitter.

Backed by 6,000 travelling Hammers in a crowd of 57,332 - a new Anfield League Cup record - the visitors simply couldn't deal with Liverpool's energy, movement and speed of play. "They were fast and quick and all over us, right from the first minute," admitted Moyes. "We never got a chance to breathe."

The only surprise was it took 28 minutes for the Redmen to make the breakthrough, but the goal was worth the wait. Harvey Elliott, playing as a right-sided forward, had already struck three shots on goal and Dominik Szoboszlai, playing right midfield, also had a couple of sighters so it was no surprise that the opener came from that side of the pitch.

Jarell Quansah won possession and brought the ball forward. He found Szoboszlai, who took a touch and had a look before hitting a rocket of a low shot that dipped enroute to the bottom corner with Areola beaten all ends up. It wasn't quite as good as his strike against Leicester City, but that's akin to saying the Ferrari isn't quite as fast as the Lamborghini.

Cody Gakpo should really have made it 2-0 before half-time when he headed Elliott's cross wide, but the chances didn't dry up - nothing was dry in the squally Anfield conditions - and when Jones got the second it was the Reds' sixth attempt on goal of the second period.

Lucas Paqueta came on for the visitors and Klopp stood Szoboszlai, Virgil van Dijk and Wataru Endo down ahead of Arsenal's Anfield visit with Alexander-Arnold, Salah and Ibrahima Konate introduced. The three subs would get a goal and three assists between them.

Salah blasted over from a tight angle before Konate made Liverpool's third when he channelled his inner Joel Matip and went on an adventure, bringing the ball deep into the Hammers' half before finding Gakpo, who rifled home a low shot from the edge of the box.

Although birthday boy Jarrod Bowen got a goal back for West

LIVERPOOL	STATS	WEST HAM
67	POSSESSION (%)	33
29	SHOTS	2
11	SHOTS ON TARGET	1
12	CORNERS	2
4	OFFSIDES	3

Ham when he finally got the better of Quansah, Alexander-Arnold - operating as a no6 - decided it was time to get his 76th and 77th assists for Liverpool, but not before Joe Gomez had an effort saved by Areola and the goalkeeper tipped a Nunez drive onto the post that was diverted wide by Salah from the rebound with the goal gaping.

Quansah tackled Paqueta and despite slipping, Alexander-Arnold played a glorious first-time through-ball that split the defence and sent Salah through to score.

As the away end emptied like the Queen Vic at closing time, Alexander-Arnold found Jones and he weaved his way into the penalty area before finding the net again and sliding towards the Kop on his knees for some long overdue adulation.

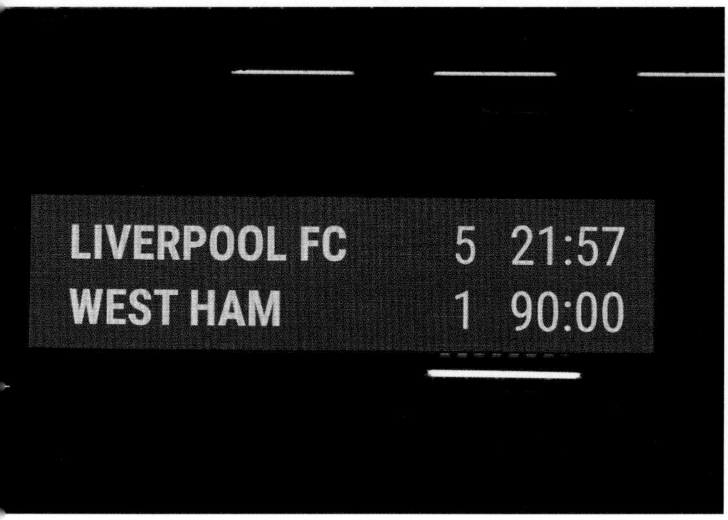

LIVERPOOL FC 5 21:57
WEST HAM 1 90:00

LIVERPOOL 2
FULHAM 1

Goals: Willian (19), Jones (68), Gakpo (71).
10.01.24 • Anfield • Attendance: 56,724
Referee: David Coote

LIVERPOOL (4-3-3): Kelleher, Bradley, Konate, van Dijk (C), Gomez, Gravenberch (Nunez 56), Mac Allister, Jones, Elliott (Gakpo 56), Jota, Diaz.
Subs not used: Alisson, Clark, Gordon, McConnell, Beck, Quansah, Nyoni.
Booked: van Dijk.

FULHAM (4-2-3-1): Leno, Castagne, Adarabioyo, Diop, Robinson, Reed (C) (Lukic 83), Palhinha, De Cordova-Reid, Pereira (Cairney 72), Willian (Wilson 72), Jimenez.
Subs not used: Rodak, Tete, Ream, Muniz, Vinicius, Francois.
Booked: Lukic, Wilson.

PRESS BOX: LEWIS STEELE, DAILY MAIL
"The theme of Liverpool's season is much like an old movie you've seen dozens of times before, the sort that pops up every Saturday night on ITV2. You know what's going to happen, the plot twist is no surprise, but you can't help but watch it again and again."

PUNDIT: JASON MCATEER, LFCTV
"Liverpool always find answers. How many times have Liverpool come back to either draw a game or take maximum points? It shows how good they are. The game as a whole was the one that I expected. They got a huge slice of luck - Curtis Jones pulling the trigger from outside the box to get it back to 1-1 - and then you felt Liverpool were always going to get that winning goal, which is what they did."

THE COMEBACK KINGS

MANAGER: JÜRGEN KLOPP
"The crowd was there with us all the time, we just didn't give them a lot to cheer in the first half. But in the second half, it was a proper, proper all-round Liverpool performance. We won the game, but it's the first leg, nothing else. It's half-time and now we go there. It's not over yet. They caused us real problems. They will cause us even more problems there."

FOR THE RECORD:
Cody Gakpo became the first Liverpool player to score in four consecutive rounds of the League Cup since Ian Rush in 1983/84.

ALSO THIS ROUND:
Middlesbrough 1-0 Chelsea →

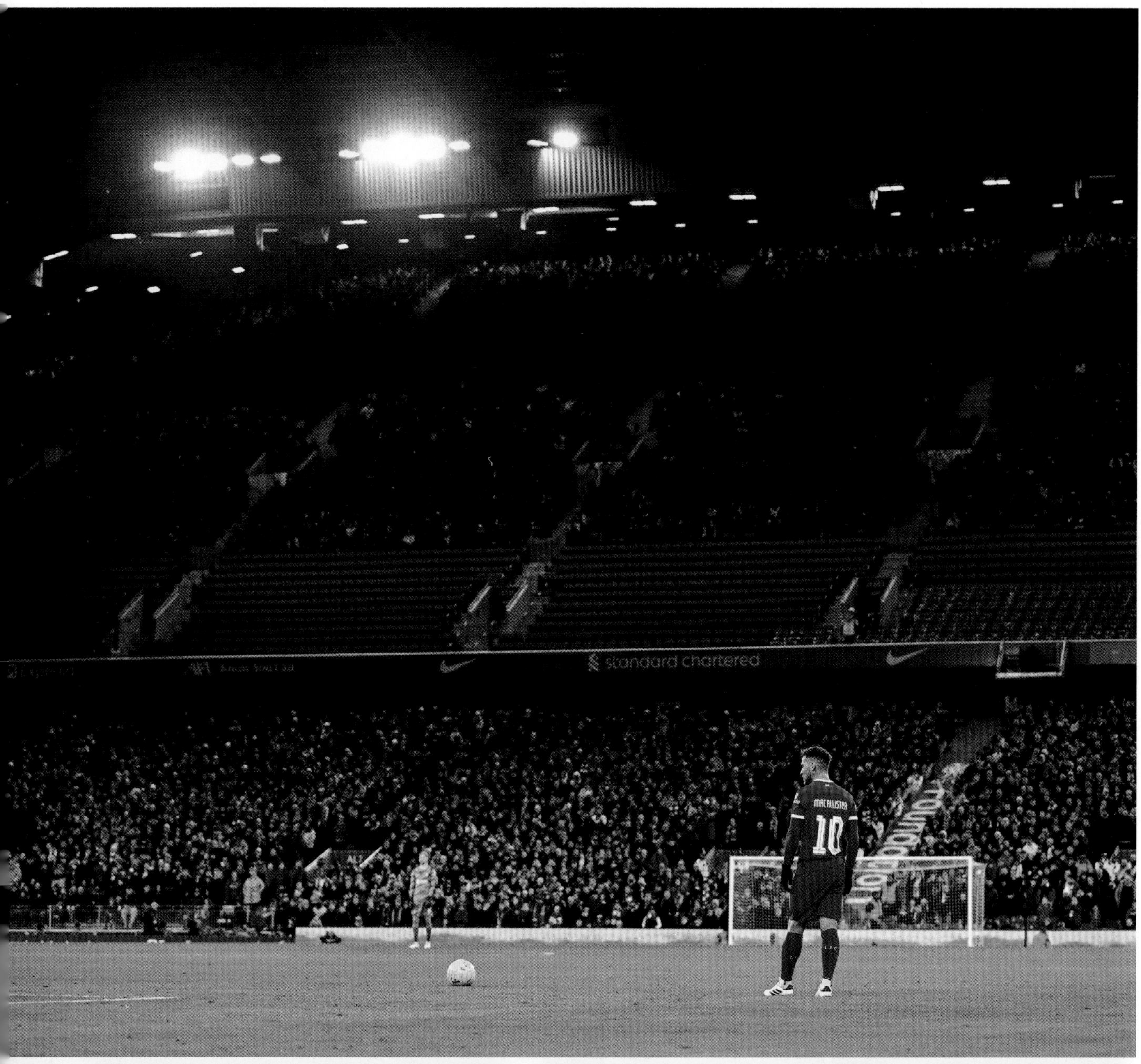

6
standard
chartered

ROBINSON
33
standard
chartered
SBOTOP

REPORT:

Winning a semi-final first leg by one goal is a bit like getting half-way through the final series of your favourite show - you just don't quite know if it will end as well as Breaking Bad or as badly as Game of Thrones.

History suggests that Liverpool's 2-1 victory over Fulham will be more Walter White than Jon Snow given the Reds have only ever been knocked out of the League Cup once after winning a semi-final first leg, but that also came after a 2-1 Anfield victory against Middlesbrough in 1997/98.

A bigger winning margin would have been ideal, but at half-time most Kopites would have settled for any winning margin. With Mo Salah, Trent Alexander-Arnold and Dominik Szoboszlai amongst the 10 players missing due to injury or international commitments, the Reds were without arguably their three most creative players. It certainly showed as Liverpool turned in a disjointed display in a forgettable first half when they created little and conceded once.

Curtis Jones had a shot comfortably saved and Diogo Jota flashed a shot across goal, but a vastly more experienced Fulham side - their youngest player was 26 compared to Liverpool's average age of 24 - making their League Cup semi-final debuts struck first.

Virgil van Dijk errors leading to goals come around about as often as Haley's Comet, but when the skipper mistimed a header it allowed Andreas Pereira to slip a pass to Willian inside the penalty area and after evading Conor Bradley's sliding challenge he fired home a low shot.

The visiting fans, unusually located next to the Sir Kenny Dalglish Stand in the lower Anfield Road end, celebrated wildly and for the 14th time this season Liverpool had conceded first. Yet maybe it was for the best.

Jürgen Klopp's 'Liverpool 2.0' seem to be at their best with their

backs against the wall as despite conceding first so often, they had only lost three of those previous 13 games.

It may be premature to start talking about mentality monsters, but producing yet another comeback to win 2-1 is indicative of a pattern rather than luck. Quite simply, this team believes it can overcome setbacks to get results.

Joe Gomez, playing at left-back on his 200th Liverpool appearance, came closest to equalising before the break with a volley into the side-netting and the Reds returned for the second stanza with more zest.

Ryan Gravenberch hit a shot just wide with Bernd Leno beaten and the Fulham keeper saved from Jones, but it was only when Darwin Nunez and Cody Gakpo emerged from the bench in the 56th minute that Liverpool truly got going.

Fulham remained a threat on the counter-attack and Kelleher had to push a Bobby De Cordova-Reid effort out, but Liverpool upped the intensity and it led to two goals in four minutes.

Had VAR been in use the Reds would surely have been awarded a penalty for handball by Antonee Robinson, who handled an Alexis Mac Allister free-kick, but referee David Coote waved play on and after Leno palmed a curler from the Argentine over Liverpool's equaliser emanated from a tackle.

Jota won a challenge against Harrison Reed, Nunez touched the ball into the path of Jones and his left-footed shot from 25 yards out clipped the elbow of Tosin Adarabioyo as he turned his back and looped over Leno. Suddenly the Reds had momentum and another tackle led to the winner.

Gomez blocked Pereira's attempted pass and the ball fell to Jones, who sent Jota forward down the left. Nunez ran in behind Timothy Castagne, received the ball from Jota and pulled it back for Gakpo, who arrived between Fulham's centre-halves and swept a sweet left-footed volley past Leno at his near post. Advantage Liverpool.

With Bradley and Gakpo causing Fulham all manner of problems down the right the Reds carved out three opportunities to get a third goal.

Jota cut across the edge of the box and fizzed a left-footed shot over before Nunez met Gakpo's cross with a brilliant header that forced Leno into a spectacular tip over. But the best chance came in the 88th minute when Bradley won a shuddering challenge on Robinson, received the ball back from Jota and clipped a perfect pass around the corner for Nunez to meet on the full only for Leno to somehow block the ball with his back leg when it looked like he'd dived over it.

Even so, the Reds had again turned a one-goal deficit into a one-goal lead to massively improve their chances of the 2023/24 Carabao Cup season finale being one to remember.

STATS

LIVERPOOL		FULHAM
67	POSSESSION (%)	33
21	SHOTS	6
7	SHOTS ON TARGET	4
8	CORNERS	2
1	OFFSIDES	1

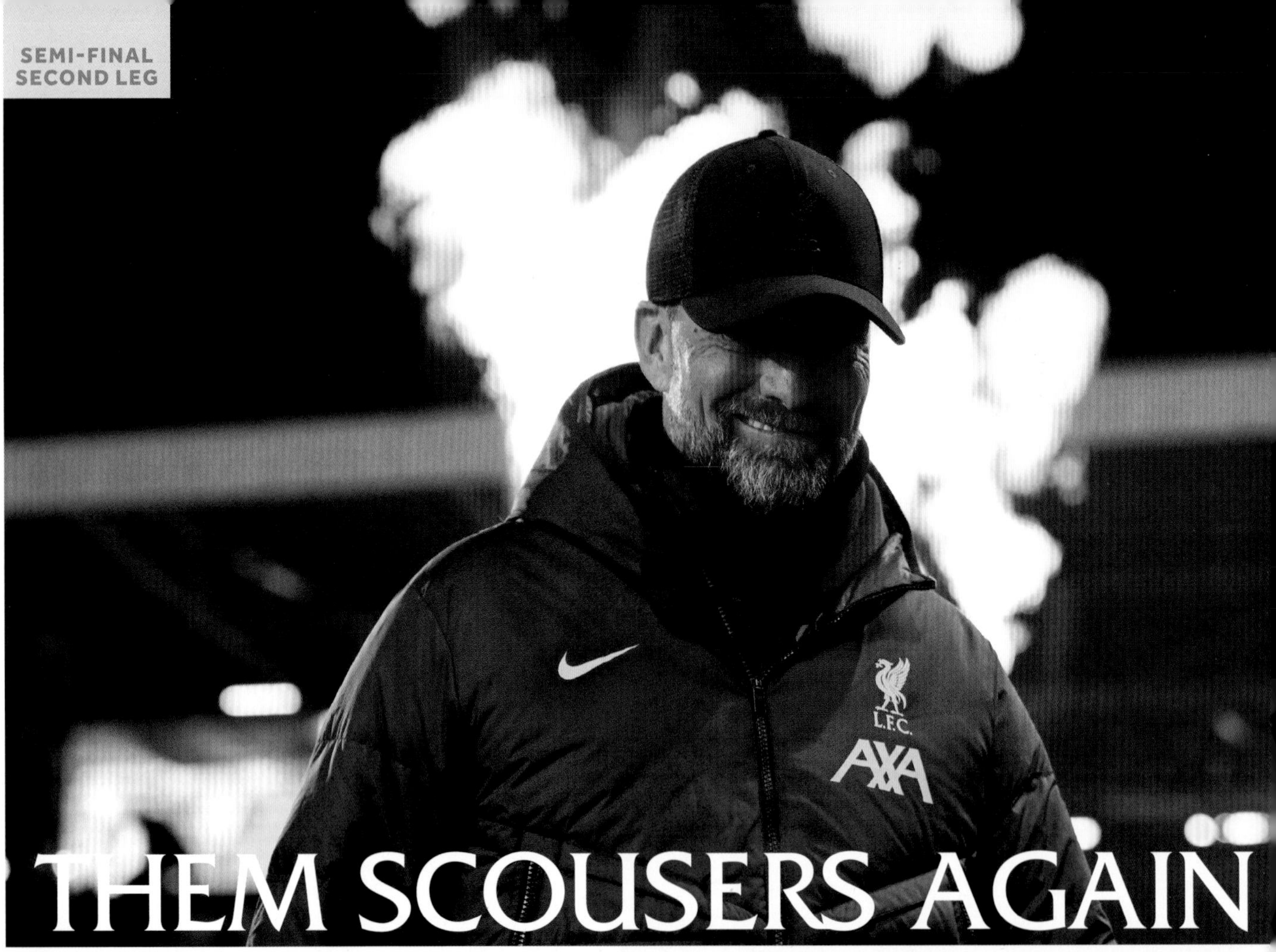

THEM SCOUSERS AGAIN

FULHAM 1
LIVERPOOL 1

Goals: Diaz (11), Diop (76).
24.01.24 • Craven Cottage • Attendance: 24,320
Referee: Simon Hooper

FULHAM (4-2-3-1): Leno, Castagne (Tete 83), Adarabioyo, Diop, Robinson, Palhinha, Cairney (C) (Reed 83), De Cordova-Reid (Wilson 67), Pereira (Muniz 83), Willian, Jimenez.
Subs not used: Rodak, Ream, Lukic, Vinicius, Francois.
Booked: Cairney, Diop, Wilson.

LIVERPOOL (4-3-3): Kelleher, Bradley, Quansah, van Dijk, Gomez, Elliott, Mac Allister (Jones 67), Gravenberch (Clark 84), Gakpo (Konate 83), Nunez (Jota 67), Diaz.
Subs not used: Alisson, Robertson, McConnell, Beck, Nyoni.
Booked: Kelleher.

PRESS BOX: JOHN CROSS, DAILY MIRROR
"They made changes, it looked a mix-and-match line-up amid a growing casualty list in the Anfield treatment room, but they still had enough quality and promising youngsters to get the job done. Jarell Quansah, 20, got the assist for Luis Diaz's opening goal while Conor Bradley did well as Klopp will have to get through this period using all of his squad. Judging by Klopp's smiles at the final whistle and the celebrations in the away end, they are enjoying the ride."

PUNDIT: DANIEL STURRIDGE, SKY SPORTS
"I think when you are warming up and preparing for these types of games, you want to make sure your first touch is good. All those types of things and you feel like 'I'm on it today'. When they were on the pitch warming up, you could see the intensity was there. They were in the moment. I had Virgil in my ear saying 'Studge move out the way man, we are trying to do passing here'."

MANAGER: JÜRGEN KLOPP
"We were just ready for this game, that's the most important thing. I told the boys I know what it means to us, but we have to show to the outside world that we want it as much as they want it. It was just a good game, a good cup game. Whoever expected tonight that we just show quality and we get through and this will be a walk in the park doesn't understand the game."

FOR THE RECORD:
Bobby Clark became the 24th player to appear in the Carabao Cup for Liverpool this season, with only Caoimhin Kelleher and Harvey Elliott starting every game.

ALSO THIS ROUND:
Chelsea 6-1 Middlesbrough

REPORT:

Luis Diaz made his Carabao Cup debut at Wembley in 2022, so perhaps it was written in the stars that he would score the goal that sent Liverpool to another final beneath the arch against Chelsea.

The Colombian was named as player-of-the-match following the Reds' penalty shoot-out victory against Fulham's West London rivals and, in his first Carabao Cup start away from Anfield since that Wembley win, was again voted the best player on the pitch after netting his first goal in this competition.

It came in the 11th minute and gave the Reds the cushion of a two-goal aggregate advantage. While there were a couple of nervy moments after Issa Diop equalised in the 76th minute, Fulham never truly looked as if they'd overturn their first leg defeat at Anfield, but Liverpool worked hard to seal their spot at Wembley.

Fulham's delayed 8,650-capacity Riverside Stand may still only be partially open, but Craven Cottage was a sea of black and white plastic flags as the two teams emerged onto the pitch and it was the hosts who had a glorious early chance to score.

Caoimhin Kelleher pushed a Timothy Castagne cross past the post and from the corner that followed Joao Palhinha found himself completely unmarked, but volleyed into the Putney End. Goalkeeper Kelleher, who along with Joe Gomez is Liverpool's current most experienced League Cup player, also did well to push a dangerous Antonee Robinson cross away from Bobby De Cordova-Reid, but after that it was the visitors who started to assume control.

Jarell Quansah sprayed a diagonal pass out to the left wing where Diaz caught the backpedalling Castagne out by leaping above him and chesting the ball down. With the full-back on the turf, Diaz cut into the box and let fly with a right-footed shot that clipped Palhinha's boot as he tried to challenge and squeezed past Bernd Leno, who pushed the ball in off his near post.

Leno beat the turf in frustration, Diaz celebrated in the corner with his teammates and *Ring of Fire* rang out from a bouncing away end. Remarkably it was also Quansah's third assist in the Carabao Cup this season and despite having fellow 20-year-old Conor Bradley playing outside him at right-back, the Reds didn't look vulnerable in that area of the pitch given their inexperience.

Indeed, it could easily have been tie over by the break. Castagne was again caught out by a diagonal pass, this time from Virgil van Dijk, that Darwin Nunez unselfishly tried to head to the unmarked Ryan Gravenberch, but he put too much on it and the ball ran away for a goal kick. Nunez also volleyed against the post, from a delightful chipped pass by Cody Gakpo, before Diaz half-volleyed the rebound in off the other upright, but the Uruguayan had strayed offside and even if VAR had been in use it wouldn't have changed the decision.

Gakpo and Gravenberch then combined to launch a five on four counter-attack with the lively Diaz the spare man, but this time Leno anticipated he'd aim for the near post again and saved easily. At the other end, Kelleher had to palm a Raul Jimenez effort away, but after the break it was Liverpool who continued to create chances.

Gravenberch won possession to send Liverpool flying forward on the counter like the Red Arrows, but when Diaz tried to tee up Harvey Elliott he played the ball behind him. Hybrid left-back Gomez attempted to get his elusive first goal, but fired over, and Gakpo also lifted an improvised flicked effort over the crossbar from a tight angle.

There was a let-off when Tosin Adarabioyo beat Kelleher to a cross and Andreas Pereira rattled the Liverpool post before another Reds counter-attack ended with Elliott shooting too close to Leno. Nunez also forced the Fulham goalie to claw away a curler and clipped a shot narrowly wide after brilliantly spinning on a sixpence.

When Diop diverted a cross from substitute Harry Wilson in with his thigh to make it 1-1 a few Liverpudlian nerves started to jangle, but after Kelleher turned a powerful Wilson shot around the post Jürgen Klopp brought on Ibrahima Konate to shore things up at the back, plus Bobby Clark to provide fresh legs in midfield.

The Fulham faithful sang 'stand up if you still believe', but the Reds held firm and that first half Diaz goal was enough to ensure it would be them Scousers again walking down Wembley Way.

STATS

FULHAM		LIVERPOOL
49	POSSESSION (%)	51
11	SHOTS	14
5	SHOTS ON TARGET	5
4	CORNERS	2
2	OFFSIDES	5

THE WINNING SQUAD

Highlighting the contributions of the 27 men and boys who played a part on the pitch to take the Reds to a tenth League Cup triumph

CAOIMHIN **KELLEHER**

Appearances: 6

Liverpool's League Cup hero of 2022 was an ever-present in the competition and a calming presence at the back. The Irish goalkeeper has made more of his appearances for the Reds (15) in the competition than any other in the current squad, level with Joe Gomez. "For me, he could play for any Premier League team. He's just a world-class goalkeeper," said assistant manager Pep Lijnders ahead of the third-round clash with Leicester City in September.

JOEL **MATIP**

Appearances: 1 Goals: 0

Assists: 0

A League Cup winner in 2022, Joel started the fourth-round win at Bournemouth ahead of his season-ending ACL injury. He played his part at the Vitality Stadium, partnering youngster Jarell Quansah, as the Reds came through testing conditions in Dorset with torrential rain and a swirling wind. His presence at the back helped see off Bournemouth's late fightback and helped Liverpool book their place in the last eight.

CONOR **BRADLEY**

Appearances: 4 Goals: 0

Assists: 0

The Northern Ireland right-back came off the bench for the final 20 minutes or so of the quarter-final victory against West Ham and then started the semi-final first leg against Fulham, delivering a player of the match performance. "I was just buzzing to get on the pitch and help the team in any way I could," he said afterwards. Played further forward in the final after the early injury to Ryan Gravenberch.

LUKE **CHAMBERS**

Appearances: 1 Goals: 0

Assists: 0

The Academy graduate came off the bench to make his senior debut in the third round win over Leicester City, replacing Kostas Tsimkas for the closing stages of the 3-1 victory over the Foxes. "I'd dreamt of that moment since I was six years old so it was very special," he later reflected. "As a young player, that's what you strive for, opportunities. I'm hungry for more, so hopefully more will come."

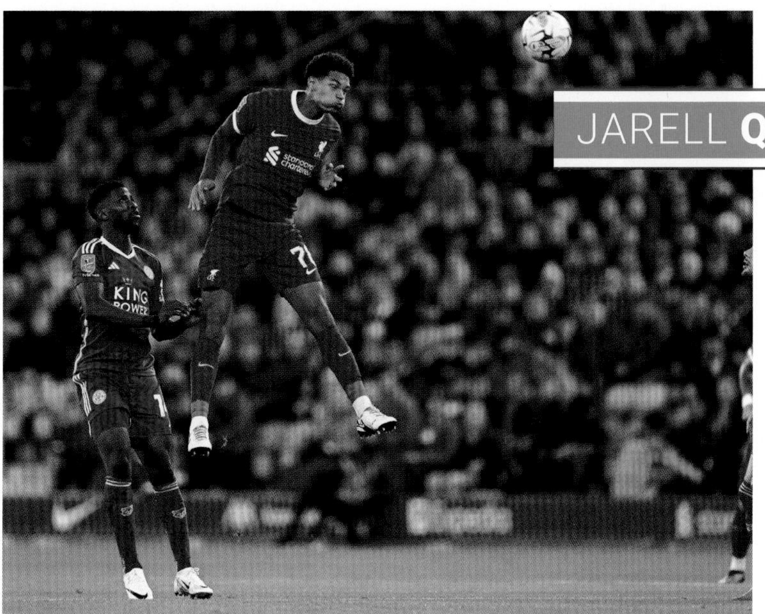

JARELL **QUANSAH**

Appearances: 5 Goals: 0

Assists: 3

The young centre-back started the Reds' first three games in this season's tournament and made a telling contribution in each outing. His display in wet and wild conditions in the fourth-round victory at Bournemouth saw him named player of the match, while at the other end of the field he supplied Anfield assists for Diogo Jota to wrap up the third round defeat of Leicester City, for Dominik Szoboszlai's early opener in the quarter-final with West Ham United and Luis Diaz's crucial strike in the semi-final at Craven Cottage. He was then the Reds' additional extra-time substitute at Wembley, coming on for Ibrahima Konate for the final 15 minutes.

JOE **GOMEZ**

 Appearances: 5  Goals: 0

 Assists: 0

The fans sang that there 'ain't nobody like Joe Gomez' and the Reds' longest-serving player brought up 200 games for the club with a solid display at left-back in the opening leg of the semi-final success against Fulham. He also started the 2-1 win at Bournemouth and the quarter-final victory over West Ham at right-back, where he also would play off the bench after 28 minutes of the Chelsea final.

IBRAHIMA **KONATE**

 Appearances: 5 Goals: 0

 Assists: 1

Ibou was ever-present at Anfield in the run to the final. As well as his commanding displays alongside Jarell Quansah and Virgil van Dijk, the no5 also provided a goalscoring assist. He was on hand to tee up Cody Gakpo to make it 3-0 on the night in the quarter-final success against West Ham United. A commanding presence for 115 minutes at Wembley before being replaced by Quansah.

VIRGIL **VAN DIJK**

Appearances: 4  Goals: 1

 Assists: 0

The skipper was on the bench for the opening two games of the tournament against Leicester City and Bournemouth but came back into the side for the quarter-final victory over West Ham United and the semi-final clashes with Fulham. Typically assured, he led by example to head home the crucial late winner in the Wembley final and was thrilled to get his hands on his first piece of silverware as Liverpool FC captain.

TRENT **ALEXANDER-ARNOLD**

 Appearances: 2  Goals: 0

 Assists: 3

The vice-captain came off the bench to truly devastating effect to help Liverpool reach the last four of the competition. At Bournemouth he provided the assist for Darwin Nunez's spectacular winner and then in the quarter-final against West Ham, another half-hour outing was all he needed to tee up Liverpool's goals number four and five for Mohamed Salah and Curtis Jones respectively. Quite an impact!

KOSTAS **TSIMIKAS**

Appearances: 4 | Goals: 0 | Assists: 1

Kostas had started the first three games in the competition before being forced to miss the semi-finals due to a shoulder injury sustained in the Premier League clash with Arsenal just before Christmas. He gave his usual all-action displays in helping the Reds reach the last four and, fit again, swung in the telling corner that led to the winning goal on his return to Wembley, scene of his FA Cup penalty shoot-out heroics in 2022.

CURTIS **JONES**

Appearances: 5 | Goals: 3 | Assists: 0

The Scouser captained the team in their opening game of the tournament against Leicester City and was deployed in an unfamiliar right-back role. "I sold the right-back idea with the captaincy, let me say it like that!" manager Jürgen Klopp later joked with reporters. Curtis performed well and made a big impact in the latter rounds with a brace against West Ham in the quarter-final and a crucial equaliser in the semi-final against Fulham.

ANDY **ROBERTSON**

 Appearances: 1  Goals: 0

 Assists: 0

The Scot made his first appearance in the tournament in the final and thought he'd produced an assist when his free-kick was headed in by Virgil van Dijk only for VAR to intervene. In the end it would be another set piece from a Liverpool left-back headed in by the skipper which proved decisive - not that Robbo was complaining as the no26 left Wembley with the eighth winners' medal of his LFC career.

WATARU **ENDO**

 Appearances: 4  Goals: 0

 Assists: 1

The midfielder featured in the Reds' first three games of the competition and supplied the assist for Dominik Szoboszlai's thunderbolt in the third-round clash against Leicester City. He also played an important role as the Reds' no6 in the wins at Bournemouth and at home to West Ham United before missing out on the semi-finals against Fulham while captaining Japan at the Asian Cup. Had "the stiffest legs I ever saw," according to Jürgen Klopp after a heroic 120-minute display in the final.

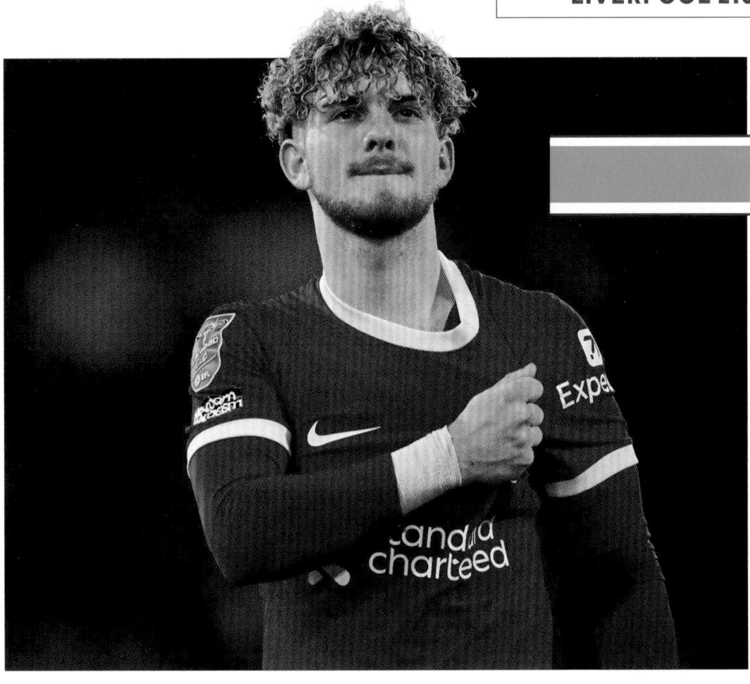

HARVEY **ELLIOTT**

Appearances: 6  Goals: 0

 Assists: 0

The 20-year-old played an important role every step of the way en route to winning the trophy, starting all six games, hitting both post and side-netting against Chelsea as the youthful Reds sought a breakthrough. He collected a second winner's medal in the tournament before his 21st birthday, having been called up to the bench following Thiago's late injury before the 2022 final against Chelsea, going on to score a penalty in the Reds' shoot-out success that day.

DOMINIK **SZOBOSZLAI**

 Appearances: 3  Goals: 2

 Assists: 0

The Hungarian captain made his mark on this season's competition with two stunning goals on the road to Wembley. His screamer against Leicester City in round three must rank amongst the hardest hit strikes at Anfield, his effort flying past Foxes keeper Jakub Stolarczyk and into the net at the Kop end. He then calmed nerves in the quarter-final against West Ham with the opening goal, another arrowed drive, this time at the Anfield Road end.

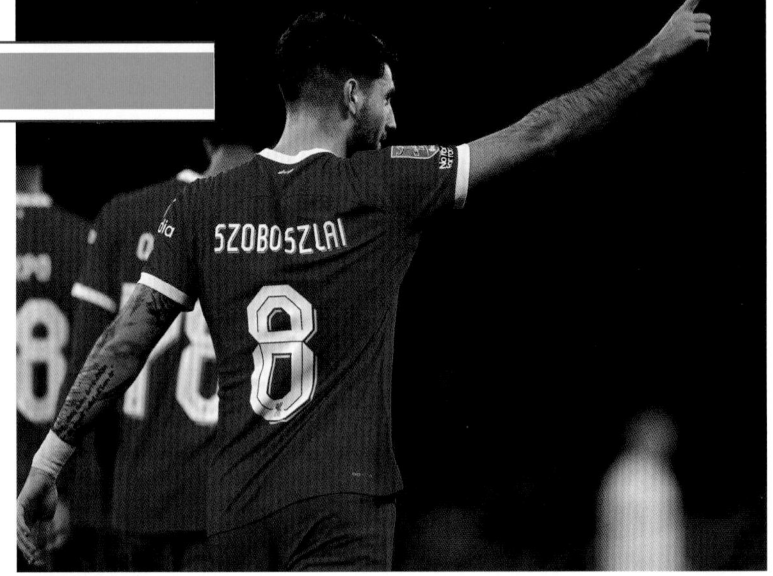

RYAN **GRAVENBERCH**

 Appearances: 5  Goals: 0

 Assists: 1

The summer signing provided the assist for the Reds' first goal of this season's tournament, teeing up Cody Gakpo for a 48th-minute equaliser against Leicester City. His clever contribution helped settle any nervous tension around Anfield after Kasey McAteer's early goal had seen the Championship side lead for 45 minutes. He then came off the bench in the win at Bournemouth, replacing Dominik Szoboszlai for the final quarter of an hour. He started the semi-final clashes with Fulham after missing the quarter-final with West Ham through injury, and was an early withdrawal against Chelsea following a challenge by Moises Caicedo that went unpunished.

ALEXIS **MAC ALLISTER**

 **Appearances: 4** **Goals: 0**

 **Assists: 0**

The Argentine was an unused sub in the third-round defeat of Leicester City but came off the bench in the next round, replacing Curtis Jones for the final half-hour of the 2-1 success at Bournemouth. Injury ruled him out of the quarter-final but he returned to start the semi-final first leg against Fulham, giving an assured display as the Reds earned a 2-1 advantage, and then played 67 minutes of the second leg success at Craven Cottage and 87 minutes of the final.

STEFAN **BAJCETIC**

 **Appearances: 1**  **Goals: 0**

 **Assists: 0**

The teenager made one of only two appearances before injury restricted his season in the third-round win over Leicester City. The midfielder came off the bench to replace Curtis Jones after 70 minutes of the Anfield encounter with the Foxes. He helped the team secure the result and was on the pitch when Diogo Jota wrapped up the 3-1 victory in the closing stages.

BOBBY **CLARK**

 **Appearances: 2**  **Goals: 0**

 **Assists: 0**

The 19-year-old returned from injury to come off the bench in the second leg of the semi-final at Craven Cottage and helped see the game out after replacing Ryan Gravenberch with 84 minutes on the clock. "Everybody sees he is ready," said manager Jürgen Klopp the following day. "That's the next step for him. Was he ready half a year ago? I don't know, but now he is and now we can bring him on and he can fill the role and make an impression. That's really good." Another impressive outing followed off the bench in the final.

JAMES **McCONNELL**

 **Appearances: 1**  **Goals: 0**

 **Assists: 0**

The teenager had been on the bench for the quarter-final win against West Ham and both legs of the semi-final against Fulham but made his first appearance in the tournament when he replaced Alexis Mac Allister towards the end of normal time. Although booked for a pull-back on Cole Palmer, the north-east native showed his promise with an assured display as the Reds' youngsters performed wonders in extra-time to see off Chelsea.

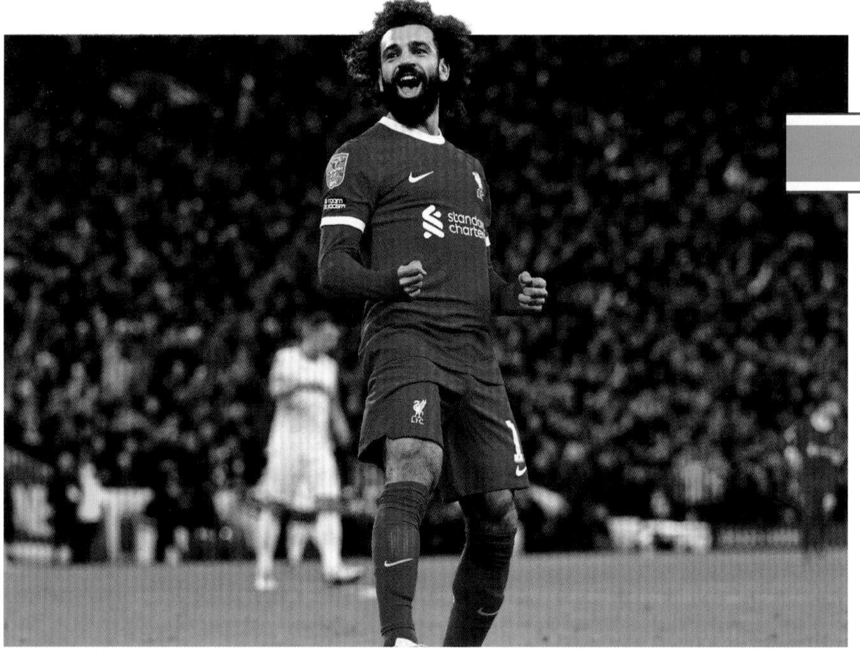

MOHAMED **SALAH**

Appearances: 2  Goals: 1

 Assists: 0

The legendary Liverpool forward started the fourth round clash at Bournemouth and then came off the bench in the quarter-final against West Ham, scoring his customary goal to make it 4-1 on the night. He found the net after being teed up in front of the Kop by Trent Alexander-Arnold with eight minutes of normal time remaining. He missed the two legs of the semi-final with Fulham, having joined up with Egypt for AFCON duty, but played his part in the Reds winning his seventh major trophy with the club.

DIOGO **JOTA**

 Appearances: 4  Goals: 1

 Assists: 0

The Portuguese attacker is another player who was integral to the Reds' success. He scored in the third round defeat of Leicester City, netting late on to seal the 3-1 victory. "The Carabao Cup was the first trophy I won with Liverpool and so it has a special place in my heart," he told the official matchday programme, reflecting on the 2022 triumph against Chelsea. "The first trophy is always special so I will always look back at that day fondly."

CODY **GAKPO**

Appearances: 6  Goals: 4

 Assists: 0

The Dutchman has played a key role in the Reds' 10th League Cup success, scoring in every round of the competition on the way to Wembley. He produced a clever finish to bring Liverpool on terms in the third round against Leicester City and then opened the scoring in awful conditions at Bournemouth in round four. He put the Reds 3-0 up against West Ham in the last eight after being teed up by Ibrahima Konate and then struck to give the Reds a vital lead against Fulham in the first leg of the semi-final at Anfield.

BEN **DOAK**

 Appearances: 1 Goals: 0

 Assists: 0

The Scottish teenager started the third round win over Leicester City and featured for the first 65 minutes of the 3-1 victory over the Foxes. Injury cut his season short but that appearance was his second start in a campaign that has seen him make five first-team outings, taking his tally to 10 since signing from Celtic in July 2022.

JAYDEN **DANNS**

 Appearances: 1  Goals: 0

 Assists: 0

Only one of two players to make his second appearance for Liverpool in a League Cup final, after Ian Rush. Prolific in the Under-18s this season, Danns had not figured for the first time until five days earlier when he made his debut off the bench against Luton Town. He performed well after replacing Cody Gakpo towards the end of normal time, seeing a powerful header tipped over the bar by Chelsea keeper Djordje Petrovic.

DARWIN **NUNEZ**

 Appearances: 5  Goals: 1

 Assists: 3

The Uruguayan scored a spectacular goal to give the Reds victory in their fourth round tie at Bournemouth and also played a pivotal part in the semi-final first leg against Fulham. Coming off the bench after 56 minutes with the Reds trailing to Willian's first-half goal, he supplied two assists within quarter-of-an-hour of coming on and helped Liverpool establish a vital lead with his contributions to goals from Curtis Jones and Cody Gakpo.

LUIS **DIAZ**

Appearances: 4 Goals: 1

 Assists: 0

The Colombian scored an important goal in the second leg of the semi-final with Fulham which helped the Reds book their trip to Wembley, producing a clever finish after being picked out by Jarell Quansah's equally impressive raking diagonal pass. The no7 also started the first leg against the Cottagers at Anfield, having previously come off the bench to replace Cody Gakpo as a late second-half substitute in the quarter-final success over West Ham United before his all-action, energy-sapping display against Chelsea.

LEAGUE CUP LEGENDS

From 1981 to 2022, the men who made a standout contribution to each winning final

KENNY **DALGLISH**

1981
It may have been before the 'official' man-of-the-match was awarded but Kenny got the nod from the press for his part in the replay victory against West Ham at Villa Park which saw the Reds win the trophy for the first time. His brilliant volley opened the scoring.

RONNIE **WHELAN**

1982
Ronnie was the man of the moment in 1982, driving home a late leveller to take the final against Tottenham into extra-time. He was then on hand to drill home the second after being teed up by Dalglish.

RONNIE **WHELAN**

1983
The Irishman received the nod again for his brilliant winner against Manchester United. His quick thinking and fine execution saw him net a brilliant curling shot to make it a hat-trick of LFC League Cup triumphs.

GRAEME **SOUNESS**

1984
Liverpool's captain fantastic in the all-Merseyside final, leading by example and scoring a fine winning goal as the Reds edged out neighbours Everton in a Maine Road replay.

STEVE **McMANAMAN**

1995
Macca's influence on the final was such that his name goes hand-in-hand with the occasion. His skills bedazzled Bolton and he scored a couple of brilliant solo strikes as Liverpool won it for the fifth time.

JERZY **DUDEK**

2003
Dudek pulled off a string of saves as Liverpool defeated Manchester United in Cardiff. Just a couple of months earlier the big Pole in goal had been culpable in a league defeat against United and only regained his place in the team following an injury to Chris Kirkland. It would not be the only time he would star for the Reds in a major final!

STEWART**DOWNING**

2012
The winger stretched the Cardiff defence on many occasions in this final which went all the way. He also kept his composure to score in the penalty shoot-out which eventually saw the Reds emerge victorious.

LFC LEAGUE CUP APPEARANCES

Ian Rush 78
Bruce Grobbelaar 70
Alan Hansen 68
Phil Neal 66
Kenny Dalglish 59
Ray Clemence 55
Mark Lawrenson 50
Ronnie Whelan 50
Emlyn Hughes 46
Alan Kennedy 45
Graeme Souness 45
Phil Thompson 43
Ian Callaghan 42
Steve Nicol 42
Sammy Lee 39
Steve Heighway 38
Terry McDermott 36
Robbie Fowler 35
Craig Johnston 35
Ray Kennedy 35

LFC LEAGUE CUP GOALSCORERS

Ian Rush 48
Robbie Fowler 29
Kenny Dalglish 27
Ronnie Whelan 14
Steve McMahon 13
Danny Murphy 11
Divock Origi 11
David Fairclough 10
Steve McManaman 10
Steven Gerrard 9
David Johnson 9
Jan Molby 9
Michael Owen 9
Graeme Souness 9

ROBBIE **FOWLER**

2001
A brilliant dipping volley from Fowler illuminated this final in Cardiff. He also kept his composure to net one of Liverpool's penalties in the successful shoot-out that saw them see off the Birmingham City challenge.

VIRGIL **VAN DIJK**

2022
The Liverpool centre-back gave a typically assured display at the back as the Reds dug deep to keep Chelsea at bay. He also stepped up to convert Liverpool's third penalty in the epic shoot-out which eventually saw them triumph 11-10 to lift the trophy.

ON CLOUD NINE

Liverpool's previous League Cup triumphs have seen high drama, unlikely heroes, and plenty of memorable goals

UP AND RUNNING

1981 Liverpool 1 West Ham United 1 (aet); Liverpool 2 West Ham 1

The Reds were favourites to beat West Ham, but the Second Division side proved tough opponents for Bob Paisley's Reds.

Two hours of football at Wembley could not separate the sides, but with just three minutes of extra-time left, Alan Kennedy appeared to have won it. However, Terry McDermott handled a last-gasp header from West Ham's Liverpool-born centre-back Alvin Martin on the line in the closing stages and, in the battle of the Rays, right-back Stewart sent keeper Clemence the wrong way from the penalty-spot to send the tie to a Villa Park replay...

A fortnight later, goals from Kenny Dalglish and Alan Hansen secured Liverpool's first League Cup triumph.

RETAINING THE TROPHY

1982 Liverpool 3 Tottenham Hotspur 1 (aet)

More late drama ensued in another tense final. Spurs, the FA Cup holders, led through a Steve Archibald goal after eleven minutes, and only a goal-line clearance by Graeme Souness prevented Archibald doubling the advantage.

That intervention proved crucial when Ronnie Whelan equalised three minutes from the end. Before extra-time began Bob Paisley urged his men to stand up to show Tottenham that they weren't tired.

Whether that tactic had any effect will remain unknown, but what is certain is that Liverpool were the better side in the additional period. Whelan again and an Ian Rush effort ensured the cup was retained.

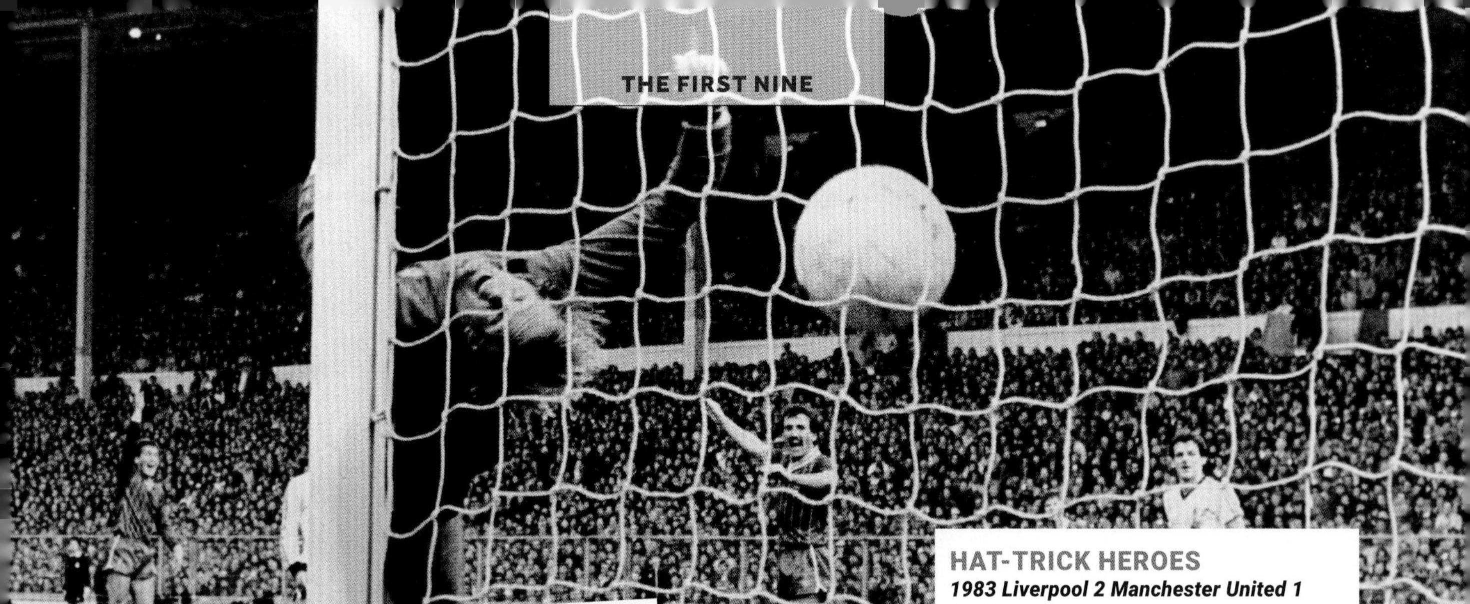

HAT-TRICK HEROES

1983 Liverpool 2 Manchester United 1 (aet)

Once again Liverpool did it the hard way, falling behind to a Norman Whiteside goal in the first half. Alan Kennedy's effort eluded goalkeeper Gary Bailey for the equaliser and the left-back later revealed how some of his team-mates were laughing when he scored because they thought his shot was so badly struck.

The by-now familiar period of extra-time eventually led to Liverpool wearing down an injury-hit United. Ronnie Whelan curled in a beautiful winner and Bob Paisley was memorably ushered up the steps by his players to collect the cup in his last Wembley final at the helm.

FOUR TOPS

1984 Liverpool 0 Everton 0 (aet); Liverpool 1 Everton 0

By the mid-Eighties Liverpool's players must have thought the League Cup final was a mandatory game of 120 minutes.

Everton edged proceedings in the first all-Merseyside Wembley final, with Alan Hansen's handling of Adrian Heath's shot on the line after just seven minutes going unpunished.

Three days later Graeme Souness was captain and match-winner in the Maine Road replay. "It was a great occasion for the city of Liverpool to have two teams in the final," he remembered. "It meant a lot to people."

THE McMANAMAN FINAL

1995 Liverpool 2 Bolton Wanderers 1

Steve McManaman bewitched Bolton with a couple of stunning solo goals as the Reds claimed a record fifth League Cup triumph.

His first arrived eight minutes before the break when he ran on to John Barnes's pass, drifted outside Alan Stubbs and inside Scott Green before side-footing past goalkeeper Keith Branagan.

Midway through the second half another successful slalom saw him ghost past Green, Jason McAteer and Mark Seagraves before curling a low right-footed shot beyond Branagan.

Alan Thompson hooked in a reply for the Football League side but it was Reds captain Ian Rush who lifted the trophy.

WORTHY WINNERS

2001 Liverpool 1 Birmingham City 1 (aet; 5-4 pens)

A tense occasion saw the Reds win the first of an eventual cup treble at Cardiff. Defender Darren Purse equalised for Birmingham after Robbie Fowler's spectacular early opener. Andy Johnson later missed the decisive penalty Jamie Carragher had scored his spot-kick moments before.

"Gerard Houllier told us that we needed to remember how winning felt and urged us to use it as an inspiration," Carragher said. "It was and we did."

JERZY'S BOYS

2003 Liverpool 2 Manchester United 0

Liverpool clinched their seventh League Cup final win at the Millennium Stadium in Cardiff thanks to goals from Steven Gerrard and Michael Owen.

Goalkeeper Jerzy Dudek, who made some costly errors against United in a league game at Anfield a couple of months earlier, was nominated man of the match, something manager Gerard Houllier had a feeling would happen.

"I told Jerzy three days ago, 'I can feel you will be the hero'," explained the Reds' delighted boss.

BLUEBIRDS BEATEN

2012 Liverpool 2 Cardiff City 2 (aet; 3-2 pens)

Kenny Dalglish guided the Reds to their eighth League Cup triumph in a final that saw Championship side Cardiff push Liverpool all the way.

Joe Mason's first-half opener gave the Welsh side a half-time advantage which was cancelled out by Martin Skrtel on the hour-mark.

With no further scoring the game went into extra-time and Dirk Kuyt's goal seemed to have secured the silverware for the Reds. But with two minutes of over-time remaining, centre-back Ben Turner pulled the Bluebirds level and took the game to a shoot-out.

Steven Gerrard, Kenny Miller and Charlie Adam missed the first three kicks and when Don Cowie slotted home, things appeared to be going Cardiff's way. But Kuyt converted his pen and Rudy Gestede struck a post – leaving things level after three efforts each.

Stewart Downing and Peter Whittingham netted and Glen Johnson then stroked home the Reds' fifth. Anthony Gerrard, cousin of Steven, had to score to send it to sudden death but fired wide leaving Dalglish and the Reds to celebrate another piece of silverware.

JEEPERS KEEPERS!

2022 Chelsea 0 Liverpool 0 (aet; 11-10 pens)

Caoimhin Kelleher was the Reds' hero, slotting home the winning penalty in the shoot-out after his opposite number, Kepa Arrizabalaga, had missed his spot-kick after the 20 outfield players had all converted.

"I was dreaming good things last night, that we would win, but never in my wildest dreams would I have thought I'd score a penalty at the Liverpool end, the winning penalty," said Kelleher afterwards. "That's definitely class and just next level."

Both sides had gone close in normal time. Joel Matip had a 67th minute goal cancelled out by VAR for a foul by Virgil van Dijk, while a little more than 10 minutes later Chelsea attacker Kai Havertz had the ball in the net but he was flagged offside.